Running Your Own Business

For a complete list of Management Books 2000 titles,
visit our web-site at http://www.mb2000.com

Running Your Own Business

Robert Leach, FCCA
and John Dore

Revised in 1998 by Clive Steward BA (Hons), FCA

First edition published 1994 by Management Books 2000 Ltd
Cowcombe House,
Cowcombe Hill,
Chalford,
Gloucestershire GL6 8HP
Tel. 01285-760722 Fax: 01285-760708
e-mail: MB2000@compuserve.com

Second edition published 1996
This new 3rd edition published 1998

Printed and bound in Great Britain by Biddles, Guildford

British Library Cataloguing in Publication Data is available

ISBN 1-85252-267-4

Whilst every effort has been made to ensure the accuracy of the contents of this
book, no responsibility can be accepted for any financial loss resulting from action
taken (or not taken) in reliance of its contents.

Preface

A problem with business books is that the information goes out of date so quickly. Indeed, information can be out of date before you buy it. To cope with this, there is a registration form at the back of the book. By copying and completing this and sending it to the publisher, you will receive *free updates* until the next edition is planned. These updates will ensure that the book is never more than a few months old at worst.

While the book is comprehensive, inevitably it cannot cover every topic that may concern you. To cover any gaps, there is an enquiry form, which you can copy and use to send in your question for a reply.

Finally, because we believe that it is also essential to be properly trained and kept up to date, registering for this book entitles you to a discount on certain training courses provided by Dore International (whose proprietor wrote Chapter 18).

Any one of these follow-ups could easily save you more than the cost of the book.

Robert Leach

Contents

Introduction

Much advice is available on how to start and run a small business. Most of it concentrates either on the management and personal skills, or on commercial and legal information. In this book, we combine the two to give a factually based guide on most of the relevant aspects of running a business.

Chapter 1 starts with asking whether you should run a business at all. Self-employment and business management is not for everyone. This chapter helps you see whether it is appropriate for you. If you decide it is not, this may be the only chapter you read. The book will have saved you heartache and money. If you decide it is, your thinking should be clarified before reading the rest of the book.

Chapters 2 to 4 deal with the rudiments of legal form, name and premises. These are not the biggest decisions you must make, but they must be made.

Chapter 5 explains how to raise finance for your business. Chapters 6 and 7 explain how the government helps through the tax system and in other ways.

Chapter 8 explains the basic accounting requirements of a business. It aims to remove the mystique of bookkeeping, while also presenting you with some valuable management accounting tools.

Chapters 9 to 12 introduce you to the main taxes you will encounter in business.

Chapter 13 explains how the tax rules can legally be used to minimise your liability. Our updating facility will prove particularly useful in this area.

Chapters 14 to 16 explain what consideration you need to give to pension, insurance and banking arrangements.

Large books are written on the law which affects business. While this book cannot hope to be comprehensive, some of the more relevant and ignored legal points are noted in chapter 17.

Chapter 18 on human skills is written by John Dore of Dore International. It draws on his extensive knowledge of this subject as taught in his much-acclaimed courses. It enables you to get to know yourself better in order to maximise your abilities. Do not skip this chapter: it may be a little uncomfortable to compare yourself with the criteria given, but it includes the area where many business men and women go most wrong.

Chapters 19 to 21 apply the human skills factor to the areas of business management, staff management and marketing. It is only fair to point out that there are different schools of thought in these areas. The principles selected in these chapters are drawn from middle-of-the-road, mainstream received wisdom. You should not go far wrong in applying them.

Chapter 22 deals with cashflow as a subject separated from accounting. This is because of the author's view that cashflow is more than an aspect of the bookkeeping function. Cashflow is the lifeblood of every business. Ultimately, you succeed or fail simply by whether you have cash when you need it.

Chapter 23 looks in more detail at the specific implications of moving from employment to self-employment while doing basically the same work, and of buying an existing business. It briefly comments on the special factors concerning franchises, management buyouts and non-profit making organisations.

Chapters 24 and 25 comment on what to do when things go wrong or go well.

Essentially, this book is nothing more than fact and advice. I believe it is the most comprehensive single volume on the subject, with invaluable supporting services. However, this alone will not guarantee you any success. You will also need vision, energy, determination, care and realism. In those areas, I can only recommend you to apply yourself after an honest appraisal of your skills.

If you decide to go ahead with your business, I wish you every success.

Robert Leach FCCA
Epsom

1 Should you do it?

The toughest question the self-employed person ever has to ask is the first one: shall I do it? There is no instant formula to give you the answer. You may ask for advice from various sources, but at the end of the day the decision is yours alone.

There are, however, four sets of questions you should ask: one about yourself and three about your business. If any of these sets gives 'no' answers, you should seriously question whether to proceed. The four sets of questions concern:

1   you
2   your product or service
3   the finance
4   the marketing.

These are like the four legs of a chair: if any one fails, the whole chair fails.

This book generally assumes that you are starting a new business from scratch. The special provisions of buying an existing business, taking a franchise, changing from employment to self-employment, non-commercial organisations and management buyouts are considered in chapter 23. But even in such circumstances, the four sets of questions are still largely relevant.

Question 1: Are you the right person to go self-employed?

When you start, you are your most important asset. You need to evaluate that most important asset. Be neither conceited nor modest. Be honest. Consider getting a second opinion from someone whose judgement you trust, perhaps your husband or wife, or brother or sister. Ideally ask someone who already runs a business.

Do you enjoy good health?
You don't get sick pay when you are self-employed. (You may be entitled to sickness benefit, but the amount is unlikely to be sufficient.)

Are you self-motivating?
Without the discipline of catching the 7.45am train and having a boss and colleagues, will you get out of bed and get on with your work? It is very easy when you first become self-employed to find that at 11am all you have done is read the newspaper and drunk three cups of coffee.

Are you disciplined and organised?
Without external disciplines, it is very easy to become sloppy and adopt the 'mañana syndrome' where everything is put off until tomorrow.

Are you resilient?
You will be rebuffed. You will work hard for contracts that you do not get. Payments will be late. Tax officers and the bank will pester you. Other businesses will try hard for your business. And when you have dealt with all those things, something entirely unforeseen will happen. Do you have the resilience and stamina to cope?

Are you capable of hard work?
Few self-employed people work from 9 to 5 with an hour for lunch? Particularly at the start, you will probably work much longer. Even if you ran a business with fixed opening hours, you will find much work to be done outside those hours. Self-employment does not suit those who have a civil service or trade union attitude to work.

If you have a hectic social life or are heavily involved in a club, church or politics, you will have to make some hard decisions about your priorities. Also, make an honest assessment of what work is actually involved. Many who 'retired to run a guest house in

Cornwall' learned the hard way that running a guest house is not just about supervising maids and socialising with guests. It involves humping beer barrels, dealing with drunks, cleaning toilets, filling in VAT returns, covering for suddenly missing staff, seeing the health inspector and so forth.

Is your family behind you?

With all the hard work, uncertainties and disappointments of a new business, the last problem you need is domestic strife. The needs of a partner and children must be considered. A family does not have to suffer when the breadwinner becomes self-employed; it can actually improve the quality of your family life. Your family may see more of you. They may themselves become involved, giving you all a new common interest.

If you work in your home, try to have a separate room as a study, studio or workshop. Trying to work in your lounge or kitchen is asking for trouble. However, it is usually best to adopt an 'open door' policy. If your children want to tell you something, it is sometimes better for them and less disruptive for you if you let them, rather than telling them to wait.

If you cannot avoid imposing on your family life, consider what compensation you may give your family. A bunch of flowers or a romantic meal as a present for the wife from the husband who has seen little of her in recent weeks, can go a long way.

Question 2: What is your product or service?

People often have bright ideas for business. However, the idea of *what* to sell is possibly the least important element in a successful business. Fewer than 1 per cent of patented inventions are manufactured commercially. Every day businesses flourish and die in all industries.

Any goods or services which can be supplied commercially can be supplied profitably. For ideas of businesses, you can simply look at the headings in any *Yellow Pages*. Marks and Spencer sell clothes; Sainsbury's sell food. Neither product is original or novel. They succeed not in the ideas of *what* to sell, but in *how* they sell it.

It is likely that you have already answered the following questions. Ordinarily, this is the one set out of the four which should prove the least difficult. But we will ask them anyway!

How skilled are you at supplying the service or product?
Every type of business needs particular skills. Don't be misled by sayings such as 'It's as easy as running a fish and chip shop'. It takes skill to run a fish and chip shop.

If you intend to operate in an area in which you worked as an employee or for which you are professionally qualified, you will have no difficulty with this question. If it is a new area, what have you done to gain experience and acquire the skills you need?

Can your goods or services be supplied commercially?
This question is particularly relevant if you intend to turn a hobby into a business. There is a world of difference between repairing clocks, playing in a musical group or breeding puppies as a profitable sideline, and doing so to earn your living. If you do something like carving animals from wood, you usually do not cost out your time. You could spend ten hours doing it because you enjoy it, and be quite happy with £10 from a grateful friend.

If you are involved in something artistic or in breeding animals, can you bear to be parted from your work?

Are you such a perfectionist that you take too long for the item to be sold at a sensible price which properly rewards your time?

Is there enough demand for your goods or service? There is a great world of difference between doing one job a month for friends, and finding ten a week for customers.

Why will someone buy your product or service rather than
someone else's?
This is probably the 'crunch question'. You must find an aspect in which you can beat your competitors. For a shop, the determining factor may simply be location. You are the newsagent next to the railway station. You are the only hairdresser for three miles. For most other businesses, the competitive aspect is usually likely to be one of:

- better quality
- cheaper price or
- better service (including support).

Do not aim for all three. Choose one. Of the three, the first is the weakest. It is not true that the world will beat a path to the door of the man who builds a better mousetrap. Betamax is technically a superior video system to VHS, but VHS became the standard.

Do not underestimate the third. Marks and Spencer built up their reputation on quality merchandise and exchanging goods. Many of their prices are not cheap. Areas in which you can compete on better service include prompt availability, delivery, back-up, technical advice, clearly written manuals, ability to upgrade and reliable after-sales support. Do not overlook such obvious areas as clean premises and polite staff.

Question 3: Can you finance the business?

Money is the language of commerce. So this is probably the most important question of all.

Do you have sufficient start-up capital?
You need enough money to cover your initial outlay *and* to keep you going while the business builds up (unless you are buying an existing business). The amount you need is more than you think. If you think of a sensible figure and double it, you may not be far wrong. Banks do not look kindly on businesses that keep coming back for more capital. A second or third request for funds is likely to get a frostier response than if you had asked for the whole amount in one go. You are also in a difficult position if the bank does say no. Asking for the money in one go does not necessarily mean that you have to receive it in one go. You can call it down as required.

Can you always meet your bills when they fall due?
This is really the same question as the previous one. However, it is

sufficiently important to need to be asked twice. A business does not go bust because it is making a loss. It goes bust because it could not pay a bill when it was due. It is possible for a business to be trading profitably, but still go bust.

Can you make sufficient profit?
Profit is a business expense, and the most important business expense. It is wrong to see a profit as a residual item after meeting other expenses. If you cannot make a profit, you should not be in a commercial business. The amount of profit you should make must be enough to pay you:

* a fair salary for your work, plus
* a reasonable return on your capital.

A reasonable return on your capital is at least 20 per cent. If you borrow money from the bank, you will probably be paying anything from 8.5 per cent to 13 per cent (when bank rates are 6 per cent). You need a little more to compensate you for the risk factor.

If you have your own funds, perhaps from an inheritance or a 'golden handshake', you should still require a return on your capital. You are, in effect, borrowing from yourself. If you did not use the money for your business, you could invest it and be earning interest. The amount of interest you earn on money is higher according to the risk you are willing to take. For a new business under untested management, a commercial investor would expect a rate of 20 per cent to 35 per cent.

For example, if you are investing £50,000 in a business and would expect a salary of £20,000 if you did the work for someone else, your minimum profit should be:

• salary	£20,000
• return on capital: 20% (min) x £50,000 =	£10,000
• minimum profit	£30,000

Can you bear the risk?
The answer to this question is always no. But it still must be considered.

Suppose it all goes wrong, what will you lose? Your savings? Your house? Your marriage?

There is no such thing as a risk-free business. Careful management never eliminates risk. However, it can reduce the risk and minimise its consequences. One traditional business management method considers the best, most likely and worst result of any situation. There is no need at this stage to consider the best. Just make sure that the most likely is good enough and the worst not too bad.

For example, in 1988 a couple remortgaged their house to go full-time into selling exotic perfumes which they blended themselves. They sold them to their upper middle-class friends and their like. Interest rates then shot up from 7.5 per cent to 15 per cent in little over a year. Their debt repayments became huge. Their customers, also facing increased debt repayments, cut down heavily on expenditure, starting with luxuries like exotic perfumes. The couple saw their income plummet and expenditure soar. The value of their house fell. Soon the house was worth less than their debts. The bank repossessed. They were bankrupt and homeless. They were vulnerable to interest rates three times over.

A business is vulnerable to many areas including the following:

- the economy (inflation, interest rates, exchange rates)
- a change of government
- change in the law
- fashion
- technological improvements
- competition
- natural disaster (weather, fire etc)
- crime.

Identify the risks to your business. Try to quantify them. See what you can do about them. Work out their cost.

Question 4: How are you going to market your goods or services?

A poor idea well marketed is a hundred times more valuable than a good idea not well marketed. Christianity offers eternal life, yet our churches are emptying. Oxford diocese started a marketing campaign and (surprise, surprise) there was a 17.5 per cent increase in church attendance.

What am I marketing?

You need to decide whether you are selling *your* product or the product generally. Are you saying 'Buy my widget because it is better than the next chap's', or are you saying 'Buy a widget – by the way, I sell them'?

Whichever you decide on, remember that the other element will still usually need to be there. A restaurant is not just competing with other restaurants. It is competing with other eating establishments, including take-away bars. It is competing with supermarkets selling food for people to prepare themselves.

What is your USP?

USP is Unique Selling Point (or Practice). Why should people buy your product rather than someone else's, or indeed a different type of product? The USP may not be the product or service itself. It may be some related matter, such as being open on a bank holiday to sell your product.

How are you going to market?

There is a range of advertising media. The commonest are:

- advertisements in publications
- advertisements on radio or television
- mailshots
- displays at exhibitions
- telesales.

They all work. The question is which one will work the best for your business?

Summary

Having considered all the points here, ask yourself the four basic questions:

1   Am I the right sort of person to be self-employed?
2   Do I have a suitable product or service?
3   Can I finance my business adequately?
4   Can I market it?

If the answer to *any* of these questions is no, then think again.

If you decide that the answer is no, you need not bother to read the other 24 chapters in this book. We will have saved you the expense and heartache of a failed business. If you then regard this book as a waste of your money, you are definitely not the right person to go into business.

2 Legal form

What is legal form?

Legal form is the structure you use for your business. There are many types, but the commonest are:

- sole trader
- partnership and
- limited company.

The decision of which form to use depends on:

- how you intend to finance your business
- the element of personal risk you must bear
- taxation
- who else is involved and
- any legal restriction.

Many businesses, whether a sole trader, partnership or limited company, include in their name '& Co.' or '& Company'. To avoid confusion in this text 'company' always means a limited company.

The sole trader

The formalities
The sole trader is the simplest arrangement of all. You must register for paying class 2 national insurance. You may need to register for VAT. Otherwise there are generally no formalities whatsoever. You

do not have to register anywhere. You need no permission. You just start.

Note that while there are few formalities for becoming a sole trader, there may be other formalities to observe. Some occupations may only be followed by suitably qualified people, including most aspects of law and medicine.

There are other businesses for which you require a licence. These include employment agencies, betting shops, sex shops, places of entertainment, financial and investment advisers, child-minding, gunsmiths, pubs and off-licences, money lending, taxi and coach driving, hotels and restaurants.

Your business may involve you in activities for which you require licensing or registration. These include driving heavy goods vehicles, handling explosives, handling radioactive material, dumping material for other people and handling personal information on computer.

Note that none of the above lists is exhaustive. There are many other businesses and activities subject to such requirements.

If your annual turnover exceeds £50,000 a year, you must register with Customs and Excise.

If you employ staff, you must register with Inland Revenue for PAYE.

Risk

If you are a sole trader, you risk everything you own (with a few exceptions). A business debt is a personal debt. Your creditors can claim against everything you have – your savings, your home, your possessions.

This does not necessarily make you vulnerable. Creditors can only claim against you to the extent that you have run up bills that you cannot pay. If the nature of your business is such that you do not run up bills or that you can always pay them, there is no risk.

Taxation

A sole trader pays income tax under Schedule D, rather than the more restrictive Schedule E for employees. This has the advantage that the rules mean that you pay your tax up to one year after you have earned it. This depends on the date your business decides to draw up its accounts. The earlier in the tax year the larger the gap (but when you cease trading the larger the catchup for tax purposes). If your profits steadily increase each year, you are in effect receiving a free subsidy from the government.

It is only fair to point out that this valuable help to existing (pre 5 April 1994) businesses is due to end on 5 April 1997. Thereafter, profits will be taxed on a different basis which offers a reduced advantage.

Whatever profit you make is added to your other income. You pay income tax on it at whatever rate applies to you.

Value added tax
If a sole trader registers for VAT, he must charge VAT on *all* his supplies made in the way of business, even if they have nothing to do with the business. A sub-postmaster invented a package identification system for which he was paid a fee. Even though this was nothing to do with his work as a sub-postmaster, *he* was registered and the supply was made in the course of business. Therefore he had to pay VAT on the fee.

Suitability
A sole trader is a suitable venue for a simple business, which does not involve anyone else to any real degree. For tax and administration purposes, it is often advisable to start as a sole trader and consider becoming a limited company when profits and liabilities are sufficiently high.

Partnership

Nature
A partnership is not a legal identity in its own right in England, Wales or Northern Ireland. It *is* a legal identity in its own right in Scotland, which has a different legal system. Under English law, a partnership is 'persons carrying on a business in common with a view of profit' (Partnership Act 1890 s1). Note that you can be in a partnership even if you do not actually succeed in making any profit.

For income tax purposes only, there is no requirement to work towards a profit.

Some professionals, such as accountants and lawyers, may trade only as sole traders or partnerships. Except for such professional partnerships, there is generally a limit of 20 partners. Partnerships are generally regulated by the Partnerships Act 1890. It is one of the few areas of commercial law hardly to have changed in over a hundred years.

Formalities

There are no formalities needed to establish a partnership. Indeed, many people may be in partnerships without realising it.

It is, however, usual to draw up a partnership agreement, generally as a deed. The partners need to determine their profit-sharing ratios, their salaries and how much interest they are entitled to on the capital they contributed to the business. If any of these matters is left undecided, the law decrees:

- profits and losses are shared equally
- no salaries are paid and
- interest at 5 per cent accrues on the capital.

It is possible to agree a loss-sharing ratio which is different from that for profits.

Tax

Income tax is payable by the partners as individuals, not by the partnership. This income is added to the partners' income to decide how much tax each should pay.

There is an exception in that one partner cannot make a tax loss while others make a profit. For example, Alan, Bert and Charlie in partnership make a profit of £60,000. They are entitled to salaries of £20,000, £40,000 and £60,000. They share profits in the ratio 2-1-1. If the partnership loss is £60,000, the taxable income for each partner is as follows:

	Total	Alan	Bert	Charlie
Salary	£120,000	£20,000	£40,000	£60,000
Share of loss	(£60,000)	(£30,000)	(£15,000)	(£15,000)
Taxable income	£60,000	£10,000	£25,000	£45,000
Alan's loss shared	- - - - - -	£10,000	(£5,000)	(£5,000)
Final taxable income	£60,000	nil	£20,000	£40,000

There are special rules when there is any change among the partners.

Risk

The risk in a partnership is greater than for a sole trader. Not only do you risk losing everything, you allow your partners to lose it for you. You can be diligent, competent and honest, and still lose everything from the carelessness of a partner. You can not, from 6 April 1997, be liable for his tax. However there is a 'joint and several' liability for any other debts of the partnership. That means if the partnership owes money, the person to whom the money is owed may sue any partner or partners he wishes.

Suitability

In most cases, the high risk of a partnership should be avoided. A partnership is like a marriage without the romance. And one in three marriages fail.

Ask yourself whether you are prepared to make your partner a signatory to your bank account. Are you prepared to let him or her have a key to your house? These are fair indications of the amount of trust you must have in your partner.

The benefits of partnership without the risk can often be achieved by remaining as sole traders and forming a contractual relationship or a loose association.

Limited company

Nature

Unlike a sole trader or English partnership, a limited company has a legal identity of its own. All its shareholders and directors can die, but the company will live on.

Forming a company is the commercial equivalent to having a baby. Like a baby, it starts with a brief but pleasurable moment of conception. This is followed by an increasingly uncomfortable pregnancy until the business gets going. It is then helpless and dependent upon you until, hopefully, it gains strength of its own and becomes independent of you. It can then form subsidiary companies and you become a 'grandfather'.

Formalities

The formalities for forming a limited company are substantial. There is a large body of law to be observed, particularly Companies Acts 1985 and 1989. The following is only the briefest of summaries of company law.

The company has members, which almost always means shareholders. From 15 July 1992, you may form a special 'single-member company' with yourself as sole shareholder. Otherwise you must have at least two shareholders. Each shareholder must contribute some money for their shares. Usually this is a nominal amount, often one share each of £1.

The company must be registered. Usually a company registration agent is used. The cost is around £100. The company is either acquired ready-made or is made for you. It you have a name which you want to use, the latter option is preferable.

On incorporation, the company is given a registration certificate with a number.

The company has a memorandum of association and articles of association. The memorandum is a form of contract with the world in general. It sets out the objects for which the company is formed and for which it may trade. (In practice this consists of several pages of legal rigmarole which mean that the company can do whatever it likes.) The articles of association are a form of contract between the shareholders. The articles are generally based on Table A produced by the government.

It must appoint at least one director and a secretary. A director may be the secretary, except that a sole director cannot be the secretary.

A company usually receives a seal, though this is no longer a requirement. The seal makes an impression on paper. It is used on certain legal documents, though signatures alone are now sufficient for all purposes under company law.

The company must, in most instances, appoint (and pay) an auditor and produce annual accounts. From 1994 certain specified companies no longer need to appoint an auditor. These are mainly the smaller owner/manager company with turnover below £350,000 and a balance sheet of not more than £1.4 million. This effectively allows the 'one-man' business to operate with the protection of limited liability but without having to pay the expenses of an audit.

The auditor reports to the shareholders on the directors. These must be filed every year at Companies House with an annual return and on payment of a fee, currently £15. In recent years, Companies House has become very sharp in chasing up and fining companies that make late or improper returns. These accounts and returns are open to public inspection. The law has detailed provisions on what must be included.

Every year the company must hold a general meeting which all shareholders and the auditor may attend, unless it has made an elective resolution to dispense with an AGM. This general meeting receives the accounts and reports, appoints the directors and appoints the auditor. For a company where the shareholders and directors are the same people, an elective resolution is now usually made.

The company must conspicuously display its name and address at all its business premises and on certain business stationery.

Once formed, the company lives indefinitely until either liquidated or struck off the register. Some companies have been trading for over three hundred years.

Taxation
Limited companies pay corporation tax. For taxable profits up to £250,000, the rate is 21 per cent (from 1st April 1999, 20 per cent), the same as the basic rate of income tax. For profits above £1,250,000, the rate is 31 per cent (from 1st April 1999, 30%). For profits between £250,000 and £1,250,000, the rate lies between the two. For example, a company which makes £600,000 pays £163,500. This is 27.25 per cent. The amount is equal to 21 per cent on the first £250,000 and 31 per cent on the excess to £1,250,000. These figures are reviewed each year in the Budget.

Note that corporation tax is paid by the company, not by its directors or shareholders. They are only liable to tax on money they receive as salary or dividends. If the company pays salaries to its directors, they are liable to income tax on the amount paid. The company gets tax relief for salaries. This gives considerable flexibility. For example if a person is liable to income tax at 40 per cent, there is an immediate saving by leaving the profits in the company where it will attract tax at a rate between 21 per cent and 31 per cent.

Corporation tax is payable nine months after the end of the company's financial year. If the company pays a dividend to its shareholders, it must pay advance corporation tax (ACT). This is not (usually) an additional tax. It is a prepayment of the company's corporation tax. It does not increase the company's tax bill. It just makes a bit of it payable earlier. The rate of ACT is one-quarter from 1 April 1994. If £4,000 is paid as dividend in 1996/97, another £1,000 must be paid as ACT. This £1,000 is deducted from the company's corporation tax bill. ACT is payable at the end of the quarter in which the dividend is paid, unless the company's financial year-end is sooner.

Whoever receives the dividend receives a tax credit for a similar amount as the ACT. So a person who receives a dividend of £4,000 in 1997/98, also receives a tax credit for £1000. He is regarded as having received £5,000 on which £1,000 tax has already been paid. This means that if he is liable to tax at the basic rate, he has no further tax liability. The company has already paid his tax for him. However, if he is liable to tax at 40 per cent, he has a liability of £2,000 of which £1,000 is already paid. He must pay another £1,000 in income tax.

Note that from April 1999 ACT is to be abolished but dividends will be paid with a (non-repayable) tax credit of 10%. Higher rate taxpayers will not be worse off, and their additional liability will remain as in the example above.

There once was a rule whereby 'close companies', those controlled by five or fewer people, were taxed as though they had paid dividends. This law was abolished in 1989.

Risk
The only risk a shareholder usually bears in a company is the amount

invested when he bought the shares. If the shares were bought 'partly paid', he can be required to pay the rest. For example if he bought 100 £1 shares on which he had only paid 25p, he can be made to pay the other £75. In practice, partly paid shares are rare in small companies, and the amounts involved are usually trivial anyway.

A shareholder becomes personally liable for a company's debts only from six months after he (illegally) becomes a sole shareholder, or if (most unusually) the court declares the company to be a sham.

It is this 'limited liability' which makes limited companies so attractive. If the company fails, all its assets can be seized and the company cease to exist. But the shareholders' private savings, house, car, yacht and other possessions are safe from the company's creditors. The term 'limited company' is a little misleading, as the company's liability is unlimited. The limit is on the shareholders' liability.

Directors are generally not liable for a company's debts, though there are several exceptions to this rule, some of them added in the last ten years. These are:

- if the director was bankrupt or disqualified when the debt arose
- where the director has signed a personal guarantee for the debt
- if the company has been wrongfully trading or fraudulently trading
- if the director has lost money while the company is being liquidated or
- the director directs the company to commit a tort (a legal offence).

A director is also liable in the unlikely event of signing a bill of exchange, promissory note, etc without giving the name of the company, or if the transaction is *ultra vires* (this means outside the scope of what a company may do). As companies now are usually allowed to do whatever they want, this is of little consequence.

In addition, a company director is personally liable:

- to penalties for not complying with any of over 150 requirements in the Companies Acts (only a handful of which are ever enforced in practice)

- for breaches of consumer law, such as those on consumer safety and trade descriptions
- for false statements, false accounting, destroying records and similar specific criminal offences
- for certain acts designed to frustrate the company's liquidation
- for certain offences connected with tax and
- for criminal offences in which the director took part.

There are certain offences for which a person may be disqualified for up to 15 years from being a director of any company. It used to be common for a business to close down owing money and for another one, often with a similar name, to start up with the same directors. This abuse of limited liability, known as 'Phoenixism', has largely been stamped out by the new offences of wrongful trading and fraudulent trading.

Suitability
The limited company has two advantages over sole traders or partnerships:

- perpetual succession and
- limited liability.

Also, when profits are sufficiently large, tax can be saved by keeping money in the business.
  Its disadvantages are:

- the expense and effort of filing returns and preparing (when required) audited accounts, among other formalities
- the directors must pay tax (and higher National Insurance) on their personal income under Schedule E through PAYE, rather than under the more favourable Schedule D.

In deciding whether to incorporate (set up a limited company), it is necessary to evaluate properly the advantages to you.
  Perpetual succession has no advantage if there is nothing to succeed. If the company's only skill is your ability at needlework

then, when you die, the company is finished anyway as it cannot continue trading. The shares will be transmitted to whomever you decree in your will, but if the company is only worth what it has already acquired, there is no difference in dying as a sole trader. (There is a difference in inheritance tax treatment, which can be significant if large sums are left in the company.)

Limited liability has no advantage if there is no liability to limit. In the early days of a business, it is unlikely to have any substantial debts. The two likeliest large creditors of a new company, the bank and the landlord, are likely to ask for personal guarantees anyway, which negates the value of limited liability.

It is often advisable to start as a sole trader and incorporate either when the liabilities become large or when you would otherwise become liable to higher rate income tax.

Other forms

There are several other types of legal form for business entities which are briefly mentioned below.

Limited partnership
This is a partnership where one or more partners has limited liability, similar to that of a shareholder in a limited company. There must be at least one general partner whose liability is unlimited. The limited partners are not allowed to participate in running the partnership. Limited partnerships are governed by Limited Partnerships Act 1906.

Unlimited company
It is possible to form a company where the shareholders' liability is unlimited. This usually happens when the business would otherwise be caught by the limit of 20 partners. Unlimited companies generally must comply with the same rules as limited companies.

Companies limited by guarantee
Instead of having shares, it is possible for a company to be limited by guarantee. That means its members agree to contribute a certain

amount if the company goes into liquidation. They pay nothing on becoming members. The guarantees are usually for nominal sums. Companies limited by guarantee are usually non-trading companies such as charities or professional bodies.

Unincorporated bodies
It is possible for people to get together for some general purpose which requires rules and funds, but which does not comprise a partnership or company. Sports clubs and music groups are common examples. Such bodies are treated similarly to limited companies in that the members' liability is limited and any profits are subject to corporation tax payable by the body itself.

Public companies
When a company gets large, it may become a public company. This means that its shares may be sold to the public in general. A company must be worth many millions before going public. The company law requirements are much tougher than for private limited companies. The company puts 'plc' rather than 'Ltd' after its name. In the UK there are about 7,000 public companies of which about 2,000 are traded on the Stock Exchange, against nearly a million private limited companies.

Groups of companies
If company A owns more than half the shares of company B, A is said to be the holding company and B the subsidiary. Together they (and any other subsidiaries) make a group. They all exist as separate limited companies, but have the additional requirement that they must file accounts as if they were all one company. There are special provisions regarding corporation tax loss relief and ACT in a group.

Consortia
A consortium is where one company is collectively owned by two or more companies, none of whom is its holding company. There is a special corporation tax provision for loss relief between consortium members.

Trust

A trust exists whenever one person holds property for the benefit of another. A trust is run by trustees whose position is similar to company directors. Trusts rarely trade, though they often invest or own property. Company pension schemes are run by trusts.

Trade unions, friendly societies, banks etc

Many types of organisation have their own rules. Some, like trade unions and friendly societies, are outside the scope of company law. Others, such as banks and insurance companies, must comply with company law adapted for them, as well as laws which apply only to them.

Anstalt

This is a creature of Luxembourg law. It is a limited company whose ownership passes simply by handing over its title deed. There is no registration procedure, making it popular for international tax fiddling.

European Economic Interest Groupings (EEIG)

This is a brainchild born of the European Community on 1 July 1990. It is, in effect, a partnership which operates in two or more EC member states. The EEIG (pronounced 'earwig') does not itself trade, but provides a supporting role for companies that do, possibly in marketing or packaging. An EEIG is 'fiscally transparent', which means that the profits which it should not be making are taxed in the hands of whoever owns the EEIG. No one has taken much notice of EEIGs.

3 Name

What name shall I use?

In general, you are free to choose any trading name you wish. If you set up a limited company, that company must have a name which is not the same as nor too similar to that of an existing company. As over a million companies have now been registered, it can be a problem finding an acceptable name.

A partnership does not have to have a name, though it is usual for it to do so. It is common simply to take the surnames of the partners. This becomes the firm's name even when the partners change. Some accounting firms are known by the names of founders who lived a century ago.

Even a company or partnership with its own name is not obliged to use that name. It is at liberty to use a business name.

Business Names Act 1985

The Business Names Act 1985 imposes two conditions on using a business name:

- the business name must not include any prohibited words and
- the business's true name must be stated on business letters, order forms, invoices, receipts and written demands for payment. The true name must also be conspicuously displayed at all places of business.

Prohibited words include:

- 'company' or anything which implies that you are a limited company (unless you are)
- words which imply a connection with the royal family, a government department or a local authority
- words which imply a connection with certain well-known organisations (such as girl guides or Red Cross) and
- words which imply a professional qualification or skill.

If you do have a connection with a local authority or the Red Cross (or other well-known organisation), you must obtain their permission before using this in your name.

The other provision means that if John Snodgrass trades as Jolly Whizzo Services, he must use the name John Snodgrass on the documents mentioned. He does not have to disclose his real name on other documents such as advertisements, packaging, statements and door signs.

Similar names
You must not use a name which is too similar to one already used for a similar product. As there no longer is a register of trade names, this can be a problem. There is a risk that you promote your product's name only to find you must change it. It is no defence that you acted innocently and took all reasonable steps to check names in use.

If you refuse to avoid a clash of similar names, the party first using the name can bring a legal action to make a court force you. Such actions are surprisingly rare, considering the millions of names in use. Even if you have registered the company name, you could still be restricted from using it, if it is too similar to another. Thus Buttercup Margarine Co Ltd was stopped from marketing Buttercup Margarine by the unregistered Buttercup Dairy Co in 1917. The words do not have to be the same or even start with the same letter. 'Brazier Mints' was considered too close to 'Glacier Mints'.

However, no one can stop a sole trader from using his real name. Thus Mr Albert Hall was allowed to promote his orchestra despite concern expressed by a well-known London venue.

In addition, there is an offence of 'passing off' explained below.

Trade marks

A trade mark is a sign, picture, special way of writing your name or a new word. A trade mark may be applied for goods or services. You are free to use any trade mark you wish, subject to the non-similarity and passing off rules already mentioned elsewhere in this chapter.

A trade mark does not have to be registered. However, it is advisable to do so before it becomes well-known. For registration, the mark must be sufficiently different from any already registered. A search is undertaken before a mark is accepted for registration. This obviously requires much subjectivity. At what point are two pictures of cats 'sufficiently different'? However, in practice there are very few cases or disputes. Trade marks are registered at The Patent Office, Concept House, Cardiff Road, Newport, South Wales NP9 1RH (01645-500505). It costs £225 to apply to register a trade mark (including the search).

Passing off

Passing off is a tort (civil wrong) in which one product appears to be made by another business. It is not necessary that any words or trade marks be copied. If the product is packaged in a similar way so that a customer could easily be confused, there could be a tort of passing off. The aggrieved company may seek an injunction to stop you.

If you deliberately copy someone else's product, you could be committing the criminal offence of counterfeiting.

What name?

Anyone who has ever chosen a name for a baby or some new club or group knows that it can quickly lead to endless wrangling and probably a sequence of not entirely serious suggestions. The name is probably less important than you think. Some apparently inappropriate names have prospered, such as Cow Gum. So have some silly ones like Really Useful Company.

There may be an advantage in taking a name which makes you

sound 'official', such as British Nursing Agency or British School of Motoring. You may want a name which reflects your image: there is a difference between Keep On Trucking Ltd and The Horseless Traction Engine Company.

Otherwise, it is probably best to keep to something straightforward such as combining your surname with the work you do, as in Bunter Tyre Services Ltd. If you later decide you need a more wacky name, you can use it as a trade name.

4 Premises

The choices

The choices of where you work are broadly:

* working from home
* renting property or
* buying property.

Note that, wherever you work, you may have to meet requirements for your premises. There are environmental regulations concerning food preparation. There are safety regulations for all places where you employ people. There are specific provisions for shops, factories and offices, and for child-minding premises.

Working from home

Planning permission
If you work from home, you first need to consider whether planning permission is required. If you are making structural alterations to your home, such as adding on a workshop, you will almost certainly need planning permission for the building work. However, planning permission may be required for a change of use even when there is no structural alteration to the premises.

The law is given in Town and Country Planning (Use Classes) Order 1987 of which C3 (dwellinghouses) is:

'use as a dwellinghouse (whether or not as a sole or main residence):

(a) by a single person or by people living together as a family or
(b) by not more than six residents living together as a single household (including a household where care is provided for residents).'

Town and Country Planning Act 1990 s55(2)(d) allows a dwellinghouse to be used for 'any purpose incidental to the enjoyment of the dwellinghouse as such'.

Guidance is given in Planning Policy Guidance Note 4 *Industrial and Commercial Development and Small Firms*, published by the Department of the Environment in 1988. It says,

'Many small businesses are started by people working in their own homes. This will not necessarily require planning permission. Permission is not normally required where the use of part of a dwellinghouse for business purpose does not change the overall character of its use as a residence. For example, the use by a householder of a room as an office would not normally require permission. It is reasonable that, where the business use becomes dominant or intrusive, permission should be required (and may be refused), but many small businesses can be carried on from home without any serious detriment to neighbouring property.'

The following were held not to require planning permission:

- teaching music in a room set aside for the purpose
- hairdressing in a room set aside for the purpose
- a doctor whose surgery is elsewhere seeing a few patients a week
- keeping four breeding bitches and boarding up to six other dogs in a large shed in a one-acre garden.

The following were held to require planning permission which was granted:

- an architect using a room as a drawing office and studio
- operating a radio-controlled taxi service three times a week
- running a playgroup

- preparing sandwiches and salads for functions, employing three staff.

The following were held to require planning permission which was refused:

- an optician who saw eight patients a day
- devoting a room to sewing garments as an outworker.

However, it must be remembered that each case is decided on its own merits.

Planning procedure

You may always ask your local council whether you require planning permission and, if so, whether they are likely to grant it. For the former question, it can be a good idea for the question to be asked by someone else in the council's area. If the answer is positive, you can apply. If not, you have the option of carrying on without telling the council. Be careful with any comment about whether permission is likely to be granted. Such an answer is given by an officer of the council, whereas the permission will be granted by the elected councillors. They may have other reasons for refusal.

Planning permission is given by the local council who are elected by local residents. Local councils are often pro-residents and often anti-business. Remember a planning application is a matter of local politics for which you can campaign if you become aware of possible objections. You can write and ring up the councillors. You can submit petitions and letters of support. Use the words 'community', 'amenity', and 'environment' generously.

If your permission is refused, you have the right to appeal to the Department of the Environment who will appoint an inspector to decide the matter. There is a limited further appeal to the High Court. But basically you have two shots at getting the permission. You can also resubmit your application supposedly amended to deal with the refusal and explain further how your plan helps the community, the environment and local amenities.

You can also ignore the council's decision. The only penalty for disobeying a planning decision is an enforcement notice which has its own appeal procedure. It can be possible to string the council along for a year or two. If they play petty politics with you, you should have no qualms about playing petty politics with them.

Nuisance
If you cause a nuisance to those near you, various actions can be taken. These include:

• private nuisance
• public nuisance and
• environmental hazard.

Nuisance can take many forms, including noise, smells, obstructing the roads and heavy traffic. Private nuisance is a civil offence; the person you have offended takes you to court. Public nuisance is a criminal offence; this arises when you disturb an entire neighbourhood.

Under new environmental laws, there are now tougher procedures for dealing with anything that causes an environmental hazard, which includes noise and most other forms of nuisance. It can be used to confiscate equipment causing the problem.

Proper accommodation
If you are working from home, it is usually essential that you have at least one room set aside for your work. Do not imagine that your daily work can be performed in the same room as used for daily family life.

Telephone
You can have extra telephone lines installed to your home. Generally they do not have to be 'business lines', though you may decide that you want them to be. A business line costs about £15 a quarter more than a domestic line. The advantages of a business line are:

• entries under the business name, in the business section in telephone directories and from directory enquiries
• a free entry in *Yellow Pages*

- priority over residential lines for repair and
- ability to reclaim VAT on telephone bills (though some reclaim may be possible on any line partly used for business). Remember that the directory entry in this case will not change. BT may become suspicious if you want to change the entry to AB Financial Services and still want to pay the lower residential rate.

However, check the costs of lines from Mercury and cable networks. All operators offer discount schemes. The one which is most beneficial to you will depend upon your own circumstances.

Income tax relief
You can claim against your income tax for the costs of working from home. Direct costs, such as furniture and business telephone lines, can be claimed in full. Other overheads, such as rent, lighting, heating, water etc, can be claimed in part. If you use one of your seven rooms for business, you may claim one-seventh of these items.

You can claim part of your council tax as an expense of your business. It is possible to claim part of the rates in Northern Ireland.

There is, in theory, a disadvantage in claiming such tax relief, because you could lose part of your main residence exemption from capital gains tax (CGT).

Capital gains tax
CGT applies to any profit you make from selling something other than in the course of business. If you sell your own home, you normally pay no CGT (on your share – if jointly owned) under the main residence exemption. However, if you have used one-seventh for business and claimed tax relief for doing so, that seventh does not qualify for relief. In practice this disadvantage can be of little consequence because of other reliefs. You pay no CGT on any gains:

- made before March 1982
- caused by general inflation up to April 1998 or
- up to £6,800 in the tax year 1998/99.

For example, you bought your house in your sole name for £20,000 in 1974. It was worth £58,000 in March 1982 and £170,000 when you sold it in March 1998. You used one-seventh for business purposes.

- The £38,000 gain before March 1982 is exempt.
- The £58,000 value at March 1982 is uplifted by a factor of 1.024 to allow for inflation during this period. The factors are published monthly by Inland Revenue. The uplift is £58,000 x 1.024 = £59,392. This is added to the original figure to give an uplifted base of £117,392.
- Your gain is £170,000 – £117,392 = £52,608. As six-sevenths qualify for main residence relief, you are only liable to CGT on £52,608 x 1/7 = £7,515.
- The annual exemption reduces this to £7,515 – £6,500 = £1,015 (relief in this example is for tax year 1997/98).
- This amount is then taxed at your marginal rate of income tax. For a basic rate taxpayer that is £1,015 x 23% = £233.
- For a mere £233 in CGT, you have been able to claim 28 years' worth of income tax relief on one-seventh of your household expenses.

Renting premises

If you cannot work from home, the next choice is usually to rent premises. The terms of a commercial lease are always a subject for negotiation between you and the landlord. But commercial leases tend to follow a pattern.

Rent is usually charged as so much per square foot or square metre. You will quickly find the going rate for your area. You need to have a clear idea in your mind of how much space you need and what it looks like. If someone says 2,000 sq ft, you need to know that is about the floor area of a semi-detached house and will accommodate about 20 people at desks with office equipment. Note the rent reviews period. The rent is fixed generally for a set number of years, and then reviewed. The review largely catches up with past inflation, so a doubling of rent after seven years, for example, is not uncommon. If you and the landlord cannot agree the new rent, you go to a rent officer who fixes it for you.

Under a commercial lease, you will usually have security of tenure. That means that the landlord cannot throw you out (except for serious offence) nor can he refuse to renew your lease when its term has expired. Usually you can only leave:

- when the lease has expired
- if you assign the lease to someone else with the landlord's consent or
- on terms agreed with the landlord.

Note that you cannot walk out at any time. You must pay the rent until the lease expires unless some other arrangement is made. When you do leave, you can be liable for restitution of the premises. This can be quite expensive. A commercial lease can be quite a financial trap.

It is common for the incoming tenant (you) to pay the legal fees both for yourself and the landlord. Sometimes the landlord may want 'key money' or a 'lease premium'. This is a single payment to let you have the lease in the first place. It is always a matter of negotiation between you and the landlord.

The lease is a long boring legal document. Do read it. Do get a solicitor to read it. It will be full of clauses saying what you can and cannot do. Most leases are based on other leases and therefore have clauses that are not always relevant. A lease for a second-floor office may have a clause saying you cannot mine for gravel. However, some clauses could restrict your business.

In particular, check your obligations and make sure you keep them. It has been known for tenants to be evicted for not cleaning the windows. Also remember that if you assign the lease to another tenant, you can be liable if that tenant defaults or goes bust.

Buying premises

Another alternative is to buy premises. Property is usually sold freehold or leasehold. In Scotland, a freehold is called a dominium utile.

Freehold means that you own the building and the land it stands on. A freehold takes the form of owning the land. This means that you automatically own what is on and under the land.

Leasehold means that you have the right to use the building to a fixed date. Then the property reverts to the freeholder. Usually there is a small charge for ground rent. A long lease is considered almost as good as a freehold, and you will pay a similar price.

Freehold and leasehold property is an expensive way to acquire property, though it has many advantages over renting. For example, you can sell when you want to. There are no unpleasant surprises at rent review and at the end of the lease. The money can be borrowed in the same way as for a mortgage of a normal house.

Land law is riddled with complications and obscure provisions. It is essential that you acquire land with the help of a solicitor.

Licence

A third way of obtaining premises is a licence to occupy. This is a less formal and more temporary arrangement than leasing. It is similar to hiring a hotel room. You are like a lodger in someone else's home. You must go when he says.

Even though the parties may agree that your occupancy is a licence, the law can sometimes construe the arrangement as a lease, giving you valuable rights should the 'landlord' want you to go when you don't.

A licence is only suitable for temporary arrangements or when alternative accommodation is readily available.

5 Raising the funds

How much?

Before working out how to fund your business, you need to work out how much you need. The answer is almost certainly more than you think. The amount is:

- all you need to spend on stock, premises, equipment, stationery, professional fees and the suchlike
- working capital to keep you going while the business gets to profit and
- some more for all the things you forgot the first time.

Of these three, the second is most commonly forgotten.

Sources

You are fortunate if you have enough money from your own resources to fund the business. It is more likely that you will need to borrow. However, lenders usually like to see that the proprietor has put in some money of his own.

The three main sources of funds are:

- bank loans
- private investment and
- investment by major funds.

Bank loans may be secured for up to £20,000, perhaps up to £50,000 if you are able to offer adequate security. There are major funds bursting with cash, but they will usually not lend less than £250,000. Some have a minimum of £500,000. Between the figures of £50,000 and £250,000 (or thereabouts), is known as the 'equity gap'. It is a difficult area in which to find investors. The only possibility is to seek private individuals with spare cash. Approaches to medium to large size accounting firms and to the various enterprise agencies will help.

Whoever's support you seek, you will need a business plan to present to them. This must be seen as a marketing exercise, just as much as the way you market your product or service. But first there are a few basic principles of investment that need to be understood.

It may also be possible to secure help from the government in some form. However, it is usually better to regard that as bunce rather than seedcorn.

Basics of investment

Risk and reward

The basic principle of investment is that the greater the risk, the greater the reward. An investor can put his money (the capital) in a building society and receive perhaps 7 per cent interest a year, with no risk to his investment. The no-risk investment becomes our yardstick.

If he puts his money into shares, which can go down as well as up, he will expect a higher return to match the higher risk. Suppose there is a 50 per cent chance that he will receive no interest at all, but no risk that he will lose his capital. He requires a 14 per cent return on the investments that succeed, so that, on average, he still makes a 7 per cent return. In practice, a risk investment attracts a premium, so perhaps 20-22 per cent is more realistic.

Investing in a new business is always a high risk, however well you may be able to present it. If it goes wrong, the investor loses all his money as well as earning no interest. He is likely to want at least 30-35 per cent return on his capital for the most likely result.

Debt and equity
There are two main ways in which someone may invest.

- debt, or
- equity.

Debt is where money is lent at a fixed rate of interest, repayable regardless of how much profit the business makes.

Equity is where money is lent for a fixed share of profits. Equity investment is most suited to limited companies, but it is possible for equity-type investment to be made in a partnership (as a limited partner or sleeping partner), or even in a sole trader.

It is possible to have both forms of investment in one business, and for the combination to be in any ratio. You may have debt of £20,000 and equity of £30,000, for example. It is also possible for a single investment to combine elements of debt and equity. For example, an investor may hold convertible debentures. This entitles him to a fixed rate of interest, but with the option of converting the debentures to shares which entitled him to a share of profits. A debenture is basically a document entitling its holder to receive money from the company other than as a share of profits, usually at a fixed rate of interest.

Another combination of debt and equity is the participating preference share. The investor is entitled to a fixed return on his capital. If the profits are good, he is entitled to a further payment related to those profits.

Note that it is possible to have an all-equity business. It is not possible to have an all-debt business. There must be at least one equity investor: one or more persons to whom all the residual profits accrue. You will be that one person, or one of them. That, after all, is why you went into business in the first place.

Gearing
Gearing is the ratio between debt and equity. The more debt there is, the more highly geared the business is said to be. The Americans call gearing 'leverage'. That term is being increasingly used in the UK.

High gearing magnifies the consequence of doing well or doing badly. This point is best illustrated with examples. Imagine a company which is funded by debt and equity totalling £100,000. It expects to make a 30 per cent profit. The debt attracts fixed interest at 20 per cent. We consider what return the equity investor gets for a low profit (15 per cent), expected profit (30 per cent) and high profit (50 per cent) when the company is low geared (£10,000 debt), medium geared (£50,000 debt), highly geared (£80,000 debt) and not geared (no debt).

	PROFIT		
NOT GEARED	Low	Expected	High
Profit earned	£15,000	£30,000	£50,000
Return on £100,000	15%	30%	50%
LOW GEARED	Low	Expected	High
Profit earned	£15,000	£30,000	£50,000
less 20% on £10,000	(£2,000)	(£2,000)	(£2,000)
available to equity holders	£13,000	£28,000	£48,000
Return on £90,000	14.4%	31.1%	53.3%
MEDIUM GEARED	Low	Expected	High
Profit earned	£15,000	£30,000	£50,000
less 20% on £50,000	(£10,000)	(£10,000)	(£10,000)
available to equity holders	£5,000	£20,000	£40,000
Return on £50,000	10%	40%	80%
HIGHLY GEARED	Low	Expected	High
Profit earned	£15,000	£30,000	£50,000
less 20% on £80,000	(£16,000)	(£16,000)	(£16,000)
available to equity holders	(£1,000)	£14,000	£34,000
Return on £20,000	-5%	70%	170%

The principle can be seen clearly if we tabulate the return for equity holders:

	PROFIT		
	Low	Expected	High
No gearing	15%	30%	50%
Low geared	14.4%	31.1%	53.3%
Medium geared	10%	40%	80%
Highly geared	-5%	70%	170%

Business plan

Purpose and scope

The business plan is a discipline which concentrates the mind on the priorities and needs of a business for the foreseeable future. While a business plan is essential when raising funds, a business plan has a wider application. It is becoming increasingly common to prepare a plan each year as an extension of the budgeting process. But here we concentrate on the plan for investment.

The plan must do three things:

• state the company's plans
• state how those plans will be achieved and
• show how that achievement satisfies the investor's requirements.

The plan must cover a clearly defined future period. This is usually three to five years. The plan includes financial forecasts. Financial forecasts are like weather forecasts: the further ahead you go, the less reliable they become.

Contents

Typically, a business plan has these contents:

1 summary (including a statement of purpose and policy)
2 background

3   details of the product or service
4   details of management and personnel
5   details of other assets and resources
6   marketing information
7   financial information
8   projected profit and loss accounts
9   timescales.

It may be necessary to include any plans, detailed accounts, statistical information or other material which support the plan rather than being part of it. They are best kept to appendices after the main report. The author recommends you consider including an extra section between 8 and 9, giving a sensitivity analysis on your financial data. Such an analysis is not often included, but can be extremely useful.

Remember that your plan is a sales catalogue for your business. It should be quietly promoting your business, even in the more turgid financial passages. Also, remember that you have little control over who reads your plan. If you have any really confidential or sensitive information, leave it out of the report or only allude to it, perhaps passing it on when you are satisfied that a particular investor really is serious. You can always see actual business plans by pretending to be an investor yourself. Business participation is advertised in *Exchange and Mart, Dalton's Weekly* and Tuesday editions of the *Financial Times*.

Summary
Always start with a brief summary on a single sheet of paper, stating in single sentences:

• how much money you want
• an indication of how much equity you are prepared to give for it, or how much interest you will pay
• the nature of the business
• the nature of the product and service
• a brief statement of why the business has good prospects.

Business and product details
In the first part, the nature of the business is explained. If a technical process is involved, give a brief summary of it. Even if the investor does not understand it, he will be pleased to see that you do. Give a brief history of your business, stressing its strong points and playing down any weak ones.

You need to answer these questions:

• what is your product or service?
• why should anyone buy your product or service rather than someone else's?
• how much will you sell it for?
• how much will it cost you?
• can you guarantee supply?
• who are you?
• why are you capable of running a business?
• what is the competition?

For example, your outline may say:

• our product is a high-speed cordless electric drill
• we can supply this for 25 per cent less than any other product on the market
• we will sell it for £40
• it costs us £20 to make each one
• we only need to buy in ten components, for each of which there are at least four suppliers
• my name is Fred Smith, I am an engineer with 20 years' experience in XYZ Machine Tools Ltd
• my partner is my brother Joe, who is an accountant who has run a small engineering works for the last three years
• we have no direct competitor for this product. Our nearest competitor is Bloggs Machine Tools who offer an industrial version of our product for £450. We believe they would not be able to compete directly because they have no experience in supplying the domestic market.

Market

The steps are:

- identify your market
- quantify your market
- calculate the penetration required
- identify methods to achieve that penetration
- cost those methods.

For example:

- our market is firms of solicitors
- there are 10,243 such firms according to the Law Society
- our projected sales require 130 to become customers, that is a penetration of 1.27 per cent
- we believe that a series of mailshots and telesales could achieve a 5 per cent success rate for the reasons given
- it will cost £40 in marketing for each new customer.

Financial statements

The best way to explain the financial prospects of a business is in management accounting terms. However, your average investor does not understand cost variance analysis, gross contribution yields, geometric progressions and probability factors.

Keep the management accounting to a minimum or omit it completely. Bank managers, corporate financiers and investors can only be relied on to understand:

- cashflow statements and
- projected profit and loss accounts.

They may not even understand them, but at least you have tried. Your cashflow statements and projected accounts will bear little relation to what actually happens. For more than two years hence, they will be complete fiction. Their purpose is to give an example of the consequences of your plan.

Always state your assumptions in any cashflow or projected accounts.

Sensitivity analysis
Although these are not usually included in business plans, a sensitivity analysis can be the most important consideration on whether to invest or even whether to set up the business at all.

You can identify the key factors to your success. There will usually be only two or three. You consider the effect on your profits if those factors differ. As profit equals revenue minus costs minus expenses, these are the three significant areas. Fixed costs and all expenses are usually not key factors in this area. You will probably need only to consider revenue and direct costs. From them you can identify the key factors.

For revenue, the key factors may be:

- response rate to marketing
- amount of repeat business
- quantity of items sold
- discounts offered or
- wastage.

For direct costs, the key factors may be:

- cost of materials
- discounts obtainable
- wastage
- reliability of labour
- deterioration in storage or
- efficient use of materials.

Having identified your two or three key factors, you consider what happens if those factors differ. For example, you assume sales of 10,000 widgets at £10 each which cost you £6 each to make. Your projected gross profit is £40,000. If your overheads are £15,000, your net profit is £25,000.

Suppose competition forces you to sell the widgets at only £8 each. Your net profit falls by £20,000 to £5,000. A 20 per cent reduction in price means an 80 per cent reduction in profit. Profit has a high sensitivity to price: the ratio is 4:1.

Suppose you only manage to sell 8,000 widgets, your profit falls by £8,000 to £17,000. A 20 per cent reduction in sales means a 32 per cent reduction in profits. Profit has a low sensitivity to sales: the ratio is 1.6:1.

Note that when you have two or more factors, you must consider them together as well as separately. If you are forced to sell widgets at £8 each *and* you only sell 8,000, your profit does not fall by £20,000 + £8,000 = £28,000 (which would give a net loss of £3,000). Your gross profit falls by £24,000 which still gives you a net profit of £1,000.

If you have a spreadsheet computer program, you can easily produce these sensitivity analyses by using the 'what if?' option. But don't get carried away with it. You only need consider two or three options for two or three key factors. You are only trying to identify the areas of sensitivity and insensitivity.

Sensitivity analysis aims to highlight vulnerable areas. However, it can also identify areas of opportunity. In our example, we know that net profit is highly sensitive to price. That means that if we can get away with increasing the price, we magnify the profit. For example, if the widgets can be sold for £12 without loss of sales, your net profit is £45,000. A 20 per cent increase in price leads to an 80 per cent increase in profits. The 4:1 ratio is now working in your favour.

Presentation

As well as considering what you say, consider how you say it. In the first stages at least, the impact of the document is governed seven times more by its appearance than by its substance. A document serves no purpose at all if it is so scruffy that no one reads it.

Your business plan is the first document your potential investor sees. Impress him. Aim for something that runs to 20 to 30 pages. Number the pages and provide an index. Do not fill the pages with solid text. Start each new topic on a new page. Use headings and sub-headings.

The document must look professional. It is not necessary to produce a printed version with full colour illustrations. Indeed something that looks like extravagant hype can be counter-productive. A neatly typed or word-processed document presented in a plastic folder purchasable from any stationer for about a pound is quite acceptable.

The bank

The bank manager does not need a full business plan, though there is no harm in supplying him with one. He is interested in the cashflow statement and what security you can offer him. He only asks two questions:

- Can the borrower repay the loan?
- How do I get the loan back if he can't?

Have answers to these questions ready before you go.

In 1991 the main clearing banks were attacked by the Office of Fair Trading for their cavalier and insensitive treatment to small businesses. They replied by saying that they had lent too generously to small business and at too low an interest rate, citing their poor returns as evidence. A more honest assessment is that the banks lost money through their head offices rather than the branches. They relied too much on the security and paid insufficient attention to profitability.

Banks also have a nasty habit of loading on charges of which you are not aware. Ask the bank:

- what interest rate applies, expressed as an annual rate (APR)
- how that rate has moved against the last few changes in banking base rate (down to 6.75 per cent in November 1998)
- how much 'arrangement fee' and similar pernicious charges they intent to make
- whether insurance is required, and if so, what the premium is and
- what security is required.

Remember that banks are only another business like you, though banks routinely behave as though they were part of the Civil Service.

Do not be afraid to haggle or shop around. The bank manager has some limited discretion in reducing costs and less in reducing rates. But you can always try another bank.

Private investors and corporate financiers

Private investors
Private investors, corporate financiers and anyone else considering an equity investment need particularly careful handling. Private investors are wealthy individuals who need to be wooed. Take them out to dinner. They will appreciate it and may pay the bill anyway. The 'more money than sense' brigade can become tiresome and even rude. They will expect you to be appreciative when they share their ignorance with you. You will probably find private investors through accountants. It may be best to let the accountant conduct most of the negotiation.

Private investors may wish to become involved in the business. You should only agree if you would be willing to taken them on as an employee in that position, even if their investment is conditional on participation. Your business is too precious to let bits of it be run as a hobby by someone with no skill. It is too precious to you to cede too much authority over running it.

Private individuals may invest under the Enterprise Investment Scheme, explained in the next chapter.

Corporate financiers
Corporate financiers are like private investors but often worse. They only lend substantial sums. Few are interested in any investment below £250,000. Many funds now start at £500,000. This is because they spend so long investigating the plan and drawing up documents that it is not worth making a smaller investment. Legal fees alone can easily exceed £10,000.

The television programme *Capital City* portrays corporate financiers as bright young things who can see instant money-making ideas in between sips of their Pimms. In reality, they have not got a clue about your business or indeed any business. They have graduated from university with first-class degrees in History, English or some other non-commercial subject, and are snapped up by banks who know of no better way to get staff. Far from seeing some instant idea, the reality is that they may have difficulty understanding your idea. Investors have reported fixations which financiers get. If you want to sell shirts in boxes, they will tell you that shirts will only sell if wrapped in Cellophane and sold with a tie, or whatever. It can take a lot of gritted teeth to deal with such people.

6 Tax help

Introduction

All political parties use the tax system to persuade people to follow their policies. As private sector commerce is now policy of all parties, there are tax provisions to help businesses.

The main tax reliefs available to industry are:

* Enterprise Investment Scheme (EIS)
* enterprise zones
* profit-related pay and share options.

Enterprise Investment Scheme

Outline
The Enterprise Investment Scheme (EIS) started on 1 January 1994. It replaced the Business Expansion Scheme (BES) which started in 1983, which in turn replaced the Business Start-up Scheme introduced in 1981.

Under EIS, an investor may buy shares in a limited company within certain limits and provided certain conditions are met. The investor is entitled to 20 per cent tax relief for money so invested. The shares are also exempt from capital gains tax on first disposal. Losses on disposal may be claimed against income or capital gains tax. From 29 November 1994, a taxable gains occuring on the sale of any assets can be deferred by subscribing for new shares under the EIS. This must be done within one year prior or three years after the disposal.

Monetary limits

The maximum an investor can invest under EIS in any tax year is £100,000. A maximum investment saves the investor £20,000 in income tax. There is no lower limit. The maximum the *company* may raise under the scheme is £1m in any tax year. If the investor invests between 6 April and 5 October (the first half of the tax year), he may offset half of his investment, up to £15,000, against his tax of the previous year.

The limits apply separately for husband and wife, so a couple can invest £200,000 in a tax year.

Qualifying conditions

To qualify, conditions must be met by the investor, the company and the shares. There are also conditions that must be met after the shares have been bought.

The investor must:

- be liable to UK income tax (but, unlike BES, does not have to be UK-resident)
- subscribe for the shares on his own behalf
- not have been connected with the company or its trade at any time before his shares were issued
- not own more than 30 per cent of the shares
- not have a spouse, ancestor or descendant who meets any of these conditions
- not make any provisions which are designed to frustrate any of these conditions

Unlike BES, an investor may be a paid director of the business under EIS.

The company must:

- trade in the UK (but, unlike BES, does not have to be UK-resident)
- carry on a qualifying trade (see below)
- not be a subsidiary
- not be a holding company unless 90 per cent or more of its

holdings qualify under EIS or are engaged in research and development.

A qualifying trade is any commercial venture except:

- trading in financial instruments
- dealing in goods other than by wholesale or retail
- banking, insurance and financial activities
- leasing, letting or receiving fees
- legal or accountancy services
- holding goods which are collected as investments
- renting private housing (allowed under BES)
- providing services to any of the above

The shares must:

- be new
- be issued after 31 December 1993
- be ordinary shares
- have no preferential rights for at least three years
- be fully paid
- not be quoted on any stock exchange

The continuing conditions are:

- the investor must generally hold the shares for five years, and
- other conditions must generally be kept for three years from when the shares were issued.

If any of these conditions are not met for the necessary time, any tax relief given on the investment will be withdrawn. For this reason, it is a normal practice for the shareholders' agreement to include a clause that an investor under such a scheme will be compensated if the company does anything which causes the tax relief to be lost.

Enterprise zones

Introduction

Enterprise zones were started in 1981 to give help to specific areas. The main help is to give increased capital allowances for capital expenditure. An area has zone status only for ten years. The reliefs stop immediately on cessation of zone status. Other help includes simplified planning procedures and concessions on rates and rent. Details of these are available from the local council.

In an enterprise zone, an initial allowance of 100 per cent may be claimed for the following items:

- industrial buildings
- shops and offices
- thermal insulation
- hotels.

If the full 100 per cent is not claimed for the tax year, a writing down allowance of 25 per cent a year may be claimed on the balance. Outside enterprise zones, a business may claim no initial allowance and a writing down allowance of only 4 per cent a year. No allowances are usually claimable for shops or offices.

The areas

The areas which have been designated as zones and are still current are given below:

Area	**expiry**
Inverclyde	2 March 1999
Sunderland: Hylton Riverside/Southwick	26 April 2000
Sunderland: Castletown	26 April 2000
Sunderland: Doxford Park	26 April 2000
Lanarkshire	31 January 2003
East Midlands: Holmewood	2 November 2005
East Midlands: Manton Wood	15 November 2005
East Midlands: Crown Farm	21 September 2005
East Midlands: Sherwood Business Park	20 November 2005
Dearne Valley	2 November 2005

East Durham	28 November 2005
Tyne Riverside no 1	18 February 2006
Tyne Riverside nos 2-7	25 August 2006
Tyne Riverside nos 8-11	20 October 2006

Profit-related pay and share options

There are six different schemes designed to promote employee participation in a company:

- profit-related pay
- profit-sharing (the 1978 scheme)
- savings-related options (the 1980 scheme)
- share options (the 1984 scheme)
- preferential share purchase
- employee share ownership plans (ESOPs).

Each of these schemes gives an independent entitlement. A person may benefit fully from more than one scheme.

Profit-related pay
An employee may receive profit-related pay (PRP) free of income tax, provided it exceeds neither of these limits.

Profit period beginning	Exempt amount
1.1.2000 onwards	Nil
1.1.99-31.12.99	Lower of 20% of earnings and £1,000
1.1.98-31.12.98	Lower of 20% of earnings and £2,000
1.1.97-31.12.97	Lower of 20% of earnings and £4,000

The PRP element must be related to the whole business or to a clearly defined part of it. Generally all employees in the business or a defined part must participate in it, though the company may exclude those who work for less than 20 hours a week or who have been employed for less than three years. The amount of PRP must be related to the business's profit or increase in profit according to a fixed formula. A PRP scheme must be registered with Inland Revenue and be audited annually. However, an employer may pay PRP beyond the limits or without registering. The requirements above are only necessary to get the tax relief. National insurance is payable on PRP.

Profit-sharing schemes
These schemes, introduced under a 1978 law, allow a company to give shares to any director or employee for them to hold for several years. The shares are held in a trust for at least two years. If the shares are disposed of after three years, no tax is paid on their disposal. If the shares are disposed of after being held for between two and three years, 100% is payable. The maximum amount that may be transferred under this scheme is limited thus:

Salary		*Maximum*
to £30,000		£3,000
£30,001 - £80,000		10% of salary
over £80,000	£8,000	

Savings-related option schemes
These schemes, introduced under a 1980 law, allow an employee to buy shares from monthly payments under a Save As You Earn scheme. The employee may subscribe up to £250 a month. Anyone who owns more than 25 per cent of the company is ineligible. The option must be held for at least three years before being exercised. The option must be to acquire the shares for at least 80 per cent of their market value when the option was granted.

Share option scheme
This most popular of schemes was introduced under a 1984 law. Until 17 July 1995 it allowed directors or employees to acquire options worth the higher of £100,000 or four times their current salary. From this date the limit is reduced to £30,000 of the value of option shares which an employee can hold at any one time. The option must be exercised between three and ten years after it was granted. An option may not be exercised more frequently than once

every ten years. The option must be exercisable for the full market value of the share when the option was granted, except that it may be exercisable for 15 per cent below market value if the company also offers a 1978 or 1980 scheme for its other employees.

Preferential share purchaser
If a company makes a public offer of shares, employees are not taxed on any additional shares they receive because they are employees. They are taxed on any discounts offered to them.

ESOPs
Employee share ownership plans (ESOPs) allow a company to set up a trust holding its shares for the benefit of employees generally.

7 Government help

Introduction

Government help has declined sharply since the 1970s. There are now few grants available to business. Those that are available are usually either linked to specific geographical areas or in commercial areas which the government wishes to promote, such as research or exports. In consequence, the schemes are an incomplete and overlapping patchwork rather than a coherent structure.

It should be noted that government help is often for short periods of time and subject to frequent change. It is convenient to consider government help under four main headings:

- assistance for geographical areas
- research and technology
- advice
- employment and training.

Assistance for geographical areas

Assistance for specific areas is provided as:

- general industrial investment
- regional enterprise grants and local authority help
- regional selective assistance
- EC loans
- factories

In addition, tax relief and exemption from rates are available in enterprise zones (see chapter 6).

General industrial investment
Under Industrial Development Act 1982 s8, a grant may be paid for major projects if:

- the project and the business are viable
- the project produces a substantial net contribution to UK output or introduces a significant degree of innovation
- the applicant can demonstrate that, but for the investment, the project would not proceed.

The amount is the minimum necessary to ensure that the project proceeds.

Regional enterprise grants
This grant takes one of two forms:

- investment grants of 15 per cent of the cost of fixed assets to a maximum of £15,000
- innovation grants of 50 per cent of agreed project costs to a maximum grant of £25,000.

The grant is available to businesses which employ fewer than 25 people for an investment grant, or 50 people for an innovation grant and are based in an assisted area, or areas of former activity in the steel and shipbuilding areas covered by RESIDER or RENAVAL respectively.

Information is also available from any DTI regional office. Outside England, businesses should contact:

Industry Department, Scottish Office
5 Cadogan Street
Glasgow G2 6AT
Telephone: 0141-248 2855

Welsh Office Industry Department
New Crown Building
Cathays Park
Cardiff
CF1 3NQ.
Telephone: 01222-825111

Department of Economic Development
Netherleigh
Massey Avenue
Belfast
BT4 2JP.
Telephone: 01232-529900

In Wales, further help is available from Welsh Department Agency. In Scotland, help is available from Scottish Enterprise. Similar help is available from Highlands and Islands Enterprise, The Development Board for Rural Wales, and Rural Areas in England and Wales.

Local authorities are allowed to help business by:

- funding building and other works
- making financial agreements with those interested in land in their area
- investing part of their pension fund in local businesses and
- disposing of land at less than market value.

Some local authorities have further financial powers to help. Details are available from the industrial liaison officer of the authority. Grants for effective use of derelict land may be obtained from the Department of the Environment.

Regional selective assistance
Regional selective assistance (RSA) applies in the assisted areas for specific projects. It is discretionary but considered against the following factors:

- the business must be viable
- it must be demonstrated that the project would not proceed if the assistance is not provided
- the project must create or preserve jobs
- the project must be judged as likely to strengthen the regional and national economy
- most of the funds must come from private sources.

Applications are made to the DTI.

EC loans

The EC will contribute up to 50 per cent of the fixed capital costs of a manufacturing industry project in qualifying areas.

Loans of £1.5m or more are provided by the European Investment Bank for industrial and infrastructure projects.

The European Coal and Steel Community provides loans to help redundant coal and steel workers. They are also held by investment divisions of British Coal and British Steel.

Factories

In certain areas, the government may provide factories on a short term 'easy-in-easy-out' basis. The rent is normal commercial rates. Plant and machinery can often be picked up at bargain prices from public auctions.

Research and technology

Help with research and technology is available in financial form from the Department of Trade and Industry (DTI) for collaborative research, pre-competitive research, and research in conjunction with academic bodies. The EUREKA system provides collaborative research grants in the EC.

Smaller firms (between 50 and 500 employees) can benefit from Support for Products Under Research (SPUR) administered by the DTI. The scheme provides grants of 30 per cent of eligible cost for projects between £50,000 and £150,000.

The DTI and Science and Engineering Research Council (SERC) jointly run training schemes linking commerce with the academic world.

ESPRIT is the EC programme to fund collaborative research in information processing, office systems and computer integrated manufacture. Brite is the EC programme to encourage basic research in new technologies by firms employing fewer than 500 employees.

British Technology Group provides finance, including equity finance, for new products and processes. The finance is usually 50 per cent of negative cashflow in return for a levy.

Advisory, information and testing facilities are provided by Laboratory of the Government Chemist, National Engineering Laboratory, National Physics Laboratory and Warren Spring Laboratory.

Advice

Many government departments produce booklets explaining matters of concern to business. In particular the Department for Education and Employment produce excellent booklets in their *Small Firms Service* and *Action for Jobs* series. Other leaflets are available from DTI, Department of Environment, Inland Revenue, Customs and Excise, Department of Transport, and Department of Social Security. Most booklets are free, well written and worth reading. Government publications improved considerably in content and presentation during the 1980s.

The DTI operate the Small Firms and Business Development Service through Training and Enterprise Councils (TECs) in England and Wales, and through Local Enterprise Companies (LECs) in Scotland.

There is no comprehensive pattern of support and guidance. To establish what is available locally contact 0800-500200 for the location of your nearest 'Business Link' office. They will be able to point you in the right direction.

Export

Guidance on exporting to Europe is available by calling 0117-944 4888.

The DTI also runs the Export Market Information Centre, Specialist Market Knowledge (with help from diplomatic staff), and a trade fair promotion scheme. The World Aid Section gives guidance on assisted supplies to developing countries. The British Standards Institution operates Technical Help to Exporters. Exports are insured through ECGD, 2 Exchange Tower, Harbour Exchange Square, London E14 9GS (0171-512 7000).

Employment and training

An unemployed person used to be able to start his own business with a weekly payment. This scheme was called the Business Start-up Scheme and previously the Enterprise Allowance. This is no longer in existence. Contact your local TEC or Business Link office.

Youth Training offers various schemes to help 16- and 17-year-olds. There is an allowance payable on top of the wages, generally £29.50 a week (16) or £35.00 (17). These have not changed since 1988. The Technical and Vocational Educational Initiative (TVEI) is intended to make the experience of all 14 to 19-year-olds in full-time education more relevant to working life.

8 Accounts

Introduction

There are three main areas of accounting:

- financial accounting – to tell you how much profit you have made
- management accounting – to tell you how you made it and
- budgeting – to work out how much you are going to make.

Financial accounting

Introduction

For day-to-day control, the only financial asset that ultimately matters is cash. In your accounts, stock and debtors are treated as 'current assets' with cash. However, you cannot spend stock or debtors. Never lose sight of the fact that cash matters. Ultimately, only cash matters.

Accounting records

For most small businesses, the only accounting book that is needed is a cash book, or two cash books – one for money that comes in, and one for money that goes out. Ensure that the former records bigger numbers than the latter.

There are many elaborate bookkeeping systems available both as books and as computer programs. They are not really needed when you start, unless you are into integrated accounting and spreadsheets. When you are larger, an integrated computer system or standard software may be appropriate. You will then be in a position to know exactly what you want, and not be prey to wizard incanting phrases like 'upgrade path' and 'IBM-compatible'.

When you computerise, you will have manuals to tell you how the system works. Computer manuals are notorious for not telling you what you need to know. However, by the time you have read them, you will be well versed enough to answer the question anyway. Save such delights for when you are established.

Accounts books are available from any large stationer for about £6 each. You keep books to record cash receipts and payments, and make any adjustments at the year-end. Each cash book should be ruled up in various columns appropriate to your business.

Receipts
The receipts book may have columns like these:

Date	Total	Name of customer	Amount	VAT	Net amount
1.4.98	469.27	ABC Engineering	368.23	54.84	313.39
		DEF Computing	101.04	15.04	86.00

These entries are repeated daily, or however frequently you bank the money. At the end of the month, you simply add up the columns. They should look something like this:

Date	Total	Name of customer	Amount	VAT	Net amount
	4,678.23		4,678.23	696.75	3,981.48

This simply means that you have received £4,678.23 in the month. Of this £696.75 is VAT and £3,981.48 is the value of goods supplied and paid for. Check your arithmetic, to see that £3,981.48 plus £696.75 does equal £4,678.23. If it does not, go through the entries until you find the mistake.

Payments
The payments book usually needs many more columns, usually at least 12.

Typical columns may be:

Date	Supplier/details	Cheque no	Amount	VAT....

Further columns analyse your expenditure under convenient headings. What these heading are will depend on your business. Typical headings may be:

- bank charges and interest
- heat, light and power
- insurance
- marketing
- postage
- premises maintenance
- raw materials
- rent and rates
- salaries and wages
- staff welfare
- stationery
- sundry
- telephone
- travel.

The final column may be marked 'other'. This is for items of infrequent expenditure which cannot be lumped under 'sundry'. Examples include legal fees, the audit fee, payments of VAT and PAYE, and the purchase of expensive equipment (fixed assets). These columns are also totalled and cross-checked each month.

Year-end
At the end of the year, you simply add up all the columns in both books. One tells you how much you received. The other tells you how much you paid. Hopefully, the latter is smaller than the former.

You can subtract your expenditure from income. This figure is not your profit, it is your *surplus* of income over expenditure (or deficit of expenditure over income). These figures must be adjusted to come to the profit figure according to normal accounting requirements. However, the income and expenditure account is more accurate and reliable than the traditional profit and loss account. Larger companies are now required to provide a form of income and expenditure account.

Profit and loss

Adjustments are made to your income and expenditure account to produce a profit and loss account. Usually you let your accountant do this, but it is useful to understand what he is doing and why.

The main change is that profit is taken earlier. If you (1) supply goods to a customer who (2) later pays you, the profit and loss account takes profit at stage (1) whereas your income and expenditure account takes it at (2), when you know you have the money. Also, if you are in the process of making, building or growing something at balance sheet date, you can take a small amount of profit then.

Another major change concerns fixed assets. These are items which are used but not consumed in the business. They include buildings, machinery, furniture and vehicles. Whereas the income and expenditure account takes the whole amount when paid, a profit and loss account takes a portion of the expenditure over the number of years you expect it to last. So if you buy a lorry for £20,000 which you expect to last for five years, you subtract £4,000 in each of the first five years' trading rather than deduct £20,000 in the first year. This £4,000 is called depreciation.

If you own freehold property, this is revalued every three years. Any increase in value is taken as profit.

The profit and loss account also treats the people who owe you money (debtors) in the same way as if they had actually paid you, and those to whom you owe money (creditors) as if you had paid them. Indeed, the account goes further to include other liabilities which have yet to arise. So if you have received goods but not yet received the invoice for them, the amount will still be deducted in your profit and loss account. Often the last two deductions made are for tax payable and the audit fee.

The final difference relates to bills for continuing services such as electricity, telephone, hire charges and road tax on vehicles. The profit and loss account ignores those bits of bills you paid this year which related to last year, and brings in the bits of this year which you pay next year. These adjustments are known as prepayments and accruals. The result of all these changes is a profit figure quite different from your surplus or deficit in the income and expenditure account. This is supposed to be more accurate. It isn't. Any second-year accountancy student quickly learns how these figures can be manipulated to give a result you want. The figure is not accepted for tax purposes for which a further set of adjustments must be made. We leave these to a later chapter.

Accounting date and reports
You must choose an accounting date. This is any day of the year to which you make up your accounts. For reasons explained later, sole traders and partnerships in the past chose 30 April. Companies usually choose the end of the month in which they were registered. The date does not have to be the anniversary of when you start.

The profit and loss account refers to a period of time, usually from the end of the previous profit and loss account (or start of trading) to your accounting date. This generally means that all but the first and last profit and loss accounts are for a period of 12 months.

A balance sheet refers to a moment in time, usually at the close of business on your accounting date. It provides two lists of figures:

• net assets and
• funding.

The net assets states the value of all that the business owns (its assets) less what it owes (its liabilities). The funding states the amount you originally put into the business (capital) plus the profit which you have not spent (retained profit). These two figures must be the same, i.e. they must 'balance'. The figure is the amount the business is worth in accounting terms. It is known as 'capital employed'. Note that if you actually sold the business, you would usually ask for a higher figure to reflect the fact that the business is earning profit. The excess of sale price over net assets is known as 'goodwill'.

Assets and liabilities
An asset is:

- money (such as petty cash and bank balances)
- things that will become money (debtors)
- things worth money (stock, work-in-progress, fixed assets) and
- things that will save money (prepayments).

A current asset is any asset which is not a fixed asset. These are cash, prepayments, debtors, work-in-progress and stock. The closer they are to cash, the more 'liquid' they are. Cash is the most liquid; stock is the least liquid. The list given earlier in this paragraph is in descending order of liquidity.

A liability is the converse of an asset. As you cannot have negative money or negative stock, the only two types of current liability are:

- things that will cost you money (creditors) and
- things which have already cost you money (accruals).

The difference between 'current' and 'fixed' is that current means an expected life of less than a year. Thus a fixed asset is one you expect to have in a year's time. A current asset is one you expect to have consumed in the year. So a vehicle is a fixed asset. Stock is a current asset. Note that the difference is based on *expectation*. The fact that you smash up the vehicle within three months but still have the stock four years later does not change its accounting treatment.

The same distinction applies to liabilities, though 'long-term liabilities' is more commonly used than 'fixed liabilities'. Current liabilities comprise almost all normal creditors. The only long-term liability now likely to be incurred is a loan.

Formats
The balance sheet follows this basic format:

    fixed assets - depreciation = net fixed assets
    current assets - current liabilities = working capital

net fixed assets + working capital - long-term liabilities =
    capital employed
original capital + retained profit = capital employed.

The profit and loss account follows this basic format:

turnover - cost of sales = gross profit
gross profit - expenses = net profit

For limited companies, the law lays down certain formats that must
be followed and requires certain information to be specifically
disclosed.

Bookkeeping
Accounts are usually kept by double-entry bookkeeping, though
there is no law or accounting requirement for any business to do so.
The basic rule here is that every financial transaction or adjustment
affects two figures. If you buy stock for cash, your stock increases
and your cash decreases. If you buy a fixed asset on trade terms, your
fixed assets increase and your creditors increase. When you pay the
bill, your creditors decrease and your cash decreases.

This is shown by debits and credits. Every transaction or adjustment involves a debit or debits and a credit or credits. The debits and
credits are always equal. Accounting has borrowed from physics to
give the law that every debit has an equal and opposite credit. An
increase in cash is a debit; a decrease is a credit. From this, other
debits and credits can be worked out.

A debit represents:

• an increase in an asset (including cash)
• a decrease in a liability
• an expense
• a loss.

A credit represents:

- an increase in a liability
- a decrease in an asset
- income
- a profit.

Whatever financial transactions or adjustments you think of can be expressed as equal and opposite debits and credits. It is possible to take figures taken from the balance sheet and profit and loss account, dividing one by the other to come to certain ratios used for comparison purposes.

Management accounting

Introduction
Management accounting is concerned with *how* you have made your profit. This is a very sophisticated branch of management and what follows is a much simplified version reducing its elements to those which are most relevant for managing a small business.

There are three types of cost accounting and the method you use depends on why you need to know the cost:

- direct costing is used to make sure that you sell the product at the right price
- marginal costing is used to make decisions about extra sales or special diversions from your ordinary business
- opportunity costing is used to make choices between competing alternatives.

Direct costing
Direct costing analyses all costs and expenses of the business into:

- direct costs and
- indirect costs.

Direct costs are those which can be related directly to the goods and service you supply. If you make an item, its direct costs are the cost of the materials bought and the labour fashioning it to turn it into your item. If you are a retailer, your direct cost is simply what you pay for the items you sell. If you supply a service, your direct costs are the labour of those who provide the service, and possibly any travel or incidental materials used by them.

Indirect costs are those which relate to simply being in business rather than to trading. Indirect costs include such items as rent, rates, inspection, heating, stationery etc.

It must be appreciated that costs do not always fall neatly into one of these two categories. For example, as you make more of an item, you may use more electricity, need more inspectors and more storage space. So such indirect costs start to become direct costs. Also, some costs may not fit into either category. For example, marketing and sales commissions can be seen as either direct or indirect. If they are substantial, it is probably more helpful to use marginal costing.

The basic principle of direct costing is that you calculate for each item you sell:

- its direct costs plus
- an apportionment of fixed costs.

For example, you make 10,000 widgets which use £10 of material and £4 of labour. Your overheads are £80,000 a year. The total direct cost of each widget is:

direct costs (material and labour): £10 + £4 = £14
apportionment of overheads: £80,000/10,000 =   £8
total direct cost: £22

This means that you must sell the widgets for more than £22 each to make a profit. If you sell your widgets for more than £22 and sell at least the number planned, you will make a profit.

If you sell more than one item, the apportionment is usually given as a percentage. For example, suppose you also intended to make 1,000 sproggets whose direct costs are £20 each. The direct costs of the items are:

10,000 widgets at £14 each =	£140,000
1,000 sproggets at £20 each =	£20,000
	£160,000

The £80,000 overheads is the equivalent of 50 per cent of the direct costs. This means that the total direct cost of the widget is 14 + 50 per cent = £21. This is £1 less than previously, because some of the overheads have been apportioned to the second product.

Direct costing ensures that you always make a profit, provided:

- your selling prices exceeds your total direct cost and
- you sell at least the number planned.

Note that it is possible to make a profit if only one of these two factors holds providing the other criterion is exceeded sufficiently to compensate. But in such circumstances, the following method is more appropriate.

Marginal costing

Marginal costing looks at the matter from a different perspective. It treats the overheads differently.

For example, assume that the widget sells for £25 and its direct cost (without any overheads) is £14. Under marginal costing, it is said to make a *contribution* of £25 - £14 = £11. The contribution is to overheads and profits. If the overheads are £80,000, you need to sell 80,000/11 = 7,273 widgets to break even. This is known as the *breakeven point*. It is the number at which you make neither a profit nor a loss.

If you make two or more items, breakeven is reached when the contributions of all items reaches the overhead. If sproggets sell for £27 and have a direct cost of £20, each sale makes a contribution of £7. Breakeven is when £11 for each widget sale and £7 for each sprogget sale reach £80,000.

Marginal costing is also used for deciding whether to accept an *additional* order. For example, you are unexpectedly offered an export order of 1,000 widgets provided you can supply them at £18 each. The total direct cost is £21, so you may be tempted to turn it down, as you are not prepared to lose £3 on each sale. However, your overheads have already been paid. You do not have to pay any more rent or rates, nor employ any more accountants because you have this order.

Suppose that your additional overheads for securing this order are £1,000. Marginal costing leads you through these steps.

- contribution per exported widget: £18 - £14 = £4
- contribution from 1,000 exported widgets: £4 x 1,000 = £4,000
- profit from export order = £4,000 - £1,000 extra overheads = £3,000.

By accepting the order, you earn an extra £3,000 in profit, even though the price is less than your total direct cost for the item.

Opportunity costing

Opportunity costing is used to make choices. A choice only ever has to be made when there is a constraint. If there were no constraint, you would not need to choose between A and B because you could do both.

The first step is to identify the choice and its constraint. Only include choices which are acceptable. Ignore choices which are unacceptable, perhaps for non-financial reasons. You may have to choose between two orders because you do not have enough material, labour or time to complete them both. You may have to choose between two stock items because you do not have enough storage space for both.

The rule for opportunity costing is that a choice is costed according to the cost of the next best alternative. It is first necessary to understand the concept of a 'sunk cost'. This is based on the simple principle that money which has been spent cannot be unspent. It is 'sunk' and therefore ignored in opportunity costing.

Similarly, costs which are common to all alternatives may be ignored. For example, a salesman wraps his company car round a lamppost. You spend £4,000 on repairs. It still fails its MOT test. The garage says it will cost £2,000 on further repairs. The car will then have a resale value of £3,000. Alternatively, they will sell you another car for £3,500. Your choice is whether to scrap the car or proceed with the repairs. The opportunity cost of buying a new car is £3,500. The opportunity cost of the repairs is £2,000. Therefore you repair the car.

Note that the £4,000 already spent on repairs is ignored. It is a sunk cost. However unwise spending that money was, you cannot unspend it. Similarly, you ignore the resale value of the car. You are not considering selling the car. If you did want to include this option, the opportunity cost is £2,000 repairs plus 3,500 for a new car, less £3,000 for the repaired car, which is £2,500. This is a better alternative than buying the car without repairing the old one, but not as good as repairing and keeping the old car.

It is unlikely that you would reach these conclusions without using opportunity costing. It is more likely that you would say, 'Good grief, I have spent £4,000 already and now I am asked to spend another £2,000. That makes £6,000. The car is not worth it. I'll cut my losses now and buy another one.' That is an attitude that will waste you lots of money.

Suppose the choice is what to do with redundant stock that you bought or made for £25,000. The choices are:

1 dump it, for a cost of £200
2 spend £4,000 on labour to turn it into a replacement for items which would otherwise cost you £10,000 or
3 sell it for £3,000 to a scrap merchant.

The opportunity costs are:

1 a loss of £200
2 a profit of £10,000 - £4,000 = £6,000
3 a profit of £3,000.

From this option (2) is clearly the best. Again, the £25,000 sunk cost is ignored. And again, it is unlikely that you would come to this conclusion without using opportunity costing.

A final application is when you have to make a loss. Our widgets have:

- a direct cost of £14
- a total unit cost of £22
- a normal selling price of £25.

The widgets have become unsellable. This can happen when an item:

- goes out of fashion
- is beaten by a competing product or
- is beaten by new technology.

Thus kipper ties, Betamax videos and gramophone needles now have little market.

Supposing the choices facing what to do with 1,000 widgets in stock are:

1 dump them, at a cost of £200
2 sell them to a scrap dealer for £1,000
3 spend £4,000 adapting them to items that will sell
   readily at £10 each.

The opportunity costs of these alternatives are:

1 a loss of £200
2 a profit of £1,000
3 a profit of £10,000 - £4,000 = £6,000.

From these, option (3) is clearly the best. Note that you do not really make a 'profit' of £6,000 at all – opportunity costs are only ever for comparison purposes. You actually make a loss of:

$$£21,000 + £4,000 - £10,000 = £15,000$$

However that is better than, say, option (1) where the loss would be:

$$£21,000 + £200 = £21,200$$

The last lesson to learn in opportunity costing is that reducing losses is as important as increasing profits. It is tempting in such circumstances to 'cut and run'. Doing so is often extremely wasteful.

Budgets and forecasts

Introduction

Although budgets and forecasts are similar in construction and appearance, they have an important difference. A forecast is a prediction of what you expect will happen. A budget is an executive order of what you have decided will happen.

If you forecast that a salesman will sell a 1,000 widgets, you are only saying that that is what you expect he will do. If you budget for 1,000 sales, that is an order which he must obey. Make sure that the difference is properly understood.

Budgets

In small businesses, it is tempting not to bother with budgets, taking the view that you will just do the best you can. Such an attitude is the first small step towards defeatism. Always set yourself a target; you may not always hit it, but having a clear view of a target considerably increases the chances of doing so.

Everyone who works for you should also have a budget, or at least some target, if their work can affect your profits. A budget is only appropriate in those areas for which someone is responsible. Thus a salesman has a sales target; a credit controller has a debt collection target; a premises manager has a cost target (the less, the better).

There is no point in having a budget for corporation tax or business rates. Inland Revenue and the local council do not work for you. In your overall budget, figures for tax and rates will appear as they go towards making up the final profit for which you (or a general manager) are responsible. However, unless there is scope for reducing them, they should not be seen as active elements in the budget.

Types of budget

The simplest type of budget is the fixed budget. There is a number or amount of money for everything. For example, the salesman is expected to sell 2,000 widgets and may only spend £1,000 selling them.

However, such an approach is not always appropriate. If you sell more widgets, you will use more material. Eventually you will incur more overheads. It is also reasonable to allow the salesman to spend more to get extra orders. For this you need a flexible budget. Under this, the cost per widget is £14 each, the salesman may spend 50p per widget sold, and so on.

Setting the budget

Always compile the budget by using the method known as zero-base budget. This means that you do *not* set the current budget as whatever last year's figure was plus a bit extra. Every item of expenditure must justify its inclusion.

Those responsible for implementing part of the budget should be consulted on the items that affect them. That does not mean that they can dictate what those items should be. It means that any arguments about achievement are sorted out before problems arise. As an organisation gets larger, the budget becomes an increasingly important commercial discipline. Start as you mean to continue.

Variance analysis

There is no point in producing budgets if no attention is then paid to them. As frequently as possible, compare the budget to the 'actual' – what has actually been achieved. Analyse the difference. This is called variance analysis. An item is reported as 'favourable' or 'unfavourable'. If the variance is of consequence, note the reason, particularly if it is the responsibility of an employee. A person should not be punished nor rewarded for a large variance without knowing the reason.

On no account revise the budget. That defeats the whole discipline of having it.

Reporting
Design a simple report. A convenient style is a single page on which basic financial and other key data are recorded. If you need reports from other people, such as when you have branches, these reports should have a similar style. Do not allow information to be withheld or presented differently, whatever the circumstances. With every completed figure report, allow a narrative report. Any unusual circumstances can be explained there.

Fix a deadline for submission or completion of the report and stick to it whatever happens, even if the report has to be issued with figures missing. Keep the deadline short. There should be little need for a report to take more than a week to complete. Keeping the deadline is a target in its own right. Non-compliance with that target should need explanation as much as any other variance.

9 Income and corporation tax

Some rudiments

Income tax and corporation tax are paid on trading profits and on most other forms of income. Income tax is paid by sole traders and partnerships. Corporation tax is paid by companies. Generally, the rules for what is allowable are the same for both taxes. The rates of tax, the allowances available and when the tax is paid differ.

The following is an outline of the two taxes. A later chapter discusses some elementary tax planning steps.

Adjusted profit

Introduction
The previous chapter explained how income and expenditure is adjusted to calculate the profit in accounting terms. For tax purposes, the profit has to be adjusted again to the 'adjusted profit' which is taxed.

The main differences between accounting profit and taxable profit are:

- disallowance of depreciation, but with possible substitution of capital allowances
- disallowance of capital expenditure, personal expenditure and other disallowed items such as most entertainment
- stock taken by a proprietor is valued differently
- disallowance of general provisions
- certain stock may need to be valued differently and
- sometimes different accounting bases are required.

When an item is disallowed, it is added back to the profit. For example if a company has a net profit of £26,000, but there are disallowed items of £3,000, its adjusted profit for tax purposes is £29,000.

Income tax is assessed under 'Schedules', some of which have 'cases'. A trader is assessed under Schedule D Case I. A vocation or profession (such as actor, author or accountant) is assessed under Schedule D Case II. There is little difference between them. Other common cases are employment (Schedule E); rents (Schedule A); dividends (Schedule F). These have different rules, particularly regarding allowability of expenses, basis periods and payment dates.

Depreciation
Depreciation is always added back. However, a capital allowance can be claimed for the following categories of capital expenditure:

- industrial buildings
- hotels
- plant and machinery
- motor vehicles
- ships and aircraft
- mines and oilwells
- dredging
- agricultural and forestry buildings
- cemeteries and crematoria
- scientific research
- patents
- know-how and
- dwellinghouses let on assured tenancies.

If an item is not within the scope of any of these, there is no capital allowance. Thus there is no capital allowance for an office, a shop, showroom or a bicycle stand.

The scope of these items is not always obvious. For example:

- industrial buildings includes docks, private roads, sports pavilions for staff, mines, warehouses, a threshing shed and buildings for catching fish or shellfish

- plant includes anything *with* which (as opposed to *in* which) the business is carried on. Court cases have decided this includes a horse, partitioning, excavation of a dry dock; swimming pool at a caravan site; decorative screens in a building society window; atmospheric lighting in a restaurant and decorative murals in a fast food shop. The law has allowed it to extend to thermal insulation; quarantine kennels; personal security equipment; private toll roads and safety at sports grounds. The Finance Act 1994 gave more detailed examples.
- motor vehicles comprises non-commercial vehicles, such as cars. Commercial vehicles, such as lorries and vans, are treated as plant.

The allowances outside an enterprise zone are:

Capital item	Annual allowance
Industrial buildings	4 per cent
Hotels	4 per cent
Plant and machinery	From 2 July 1997-1 July 1998 and 2 July 1998-1July 1999 there is available for small and medium-sized businesses a first-year allowance of 50% and 40% respectively
	For other companies the allowance is: 25 per cent on reducing balance method except 10 per cent for foreign leased assets
Motor vehicles	25 per cent on reducing balance method to a maximum of £3,000 per car (£2,000 before 6 April 1992)
Ships and aircraft	as plant
Mines and oilwells	25 per cent on reducing balance method except 10 per cent for acquisition of rights over minerals
Dredging	4 per cent
Agricultural buildings	4 per cent

Cemeteries	according to unused grave spaces
Scientific research	100 per cent in first year
Patents	25 per cent on reducing balance method
Know-how	25 per cent on reducing balance method
Dwelling houses	4 per cent

The 4 per cent annual allowances mean that the cost is spread over 25 years in equal instalments.

The 25 per cent 'reducing balance' allowances mean that you take 25 per cent of whatever is left after the previous allowance has been deducted. This means that the written down value (WDV) never reaches zero. For example if you buy a patent for £4,000, the allowances are:

cost		£4,000
allowance for year 1; 25% x £4,000	=	£1,000
written down value at end of year 1	=	£3,000
allowance for year 2: 25% x £3,000	=	£750
written down value at end of year 2	=	£2,250
allowance for year 3: 25% x £2,250	=	£563
written down value at end of year 3	=	£1,687 etc.

When an asset is sold, lost, destroyed or otherwise disposed of, any unused WDV is given as a balancing allowance. For example, if the patent above was sold after year 3 for £1,000, the company could claim another £687 as a balancing allowance. If it was sold for £2,000, the company would have to pay another £313 as a balancing charge.

Balancing charges and allowances do not apply in the same way to most plant and machinery, nor to cars which are 'pooled'. Instead, the disposal proceeds are simply deducted from the pool which continues to be written down at 25 per cent a year.

Disallowed items
The following items are not allowed for income or corporation tax purposes:

- items of a personal nature, or otherwise not connected with the business
- items of a capital nature, such as fixed assets or legal expenses in buying a business
- the drawings of a sole trader or partner, or any other payment to a partner (such as interest on capital)
- entertainment, other than of your staff
- payments of any tax, other than non-deductible VAT and class 2 and 4 national insurance
- most fines (but fixed penalties for motoring expenses are allowed)
- travel from home to work
- sums recoverable by insurance
- unjustified contingent liabilities
- medical expenses.

Gifts to customers are allowable only if each gift:

- costs less than £10 per customer
- contains a conspicuous advertisement for the business and
- does not comprise food, alcoholic drink or tobacco.

Charitable donations are allowable only if:

- made by deed of covenant or
- made under Gift Aid or
- the charity is related to the business (such as welfare organisation for ex-employees) or
- is made by a company and does not exceed 3 per cent of the amount paid as dividends.

Stock taken by proprietor
If you take a widget costing £21 and selling for £28 for your personal use, you record a 'sale' to yourself of £21 in your accounts. For tax purposes, you must deduct the full retail price of £28.

General provisions
It is common to allocate part of the profit as a 'provision'. For

example, you may provide £2,000 from a profit of £10,000 to replace an item. The profit is then restated as £8,000. Such provisions are not allowable.

If you have good reason to believe that certain customers will not pay their bills, you may provide for them as doubtful debts. Such provision is allowable. However a general provision, say of 1 per cent of all debts, is not allowable.

Stock valuation

The stock must be valued under a valid method, such as 'FIFO' (first in, first out). Net realisable value and discounted selling price can also be acceptable. Other methods such as 'LIFO' (last in, first out) are not acceptable. If LIFO or another unacceptable method is used, the stock must be revalued.

If it is realised that a long-term contract, such as a three-year building project, will make a loss, accounting standard SSAP 9 requires that loss to be reflected in the accounts immediately it is realised. Such a loss is not allowable for tax until the expenditure has actually been incurred.

Accounting bases

Sometimes accounts are prepared on the 'cash basis'. This is basically an income and expenditure account, rather than a profit and loss account. For tax purposes, the cash basis may only be used by authors, barristers or by anyone else who can persuade Inland Revenue that it gives a fair measure of their profit.

Before 6 June 1985, companies had to produce accounts adjusted for inflation. These could be used as the main accounts. Companies may still produce such accounts voluntarily. Inflation-adjusted accounts are not acceptable for tax purpose. The LIFO stock valuation method is not acceptable because it introduces an element of inflation accounting.

Income tax

Basic principle

The basis steps to working out your tax are:

- your adjusted profit for the appropriate basis period is added to your other income
- any reliefs that you may be able to claim are deducted
- deduct annual charges
- deduct personal allowances
- multiply the balance by the appropriate rates of income tax
- deduct from that any tax already paid.

The tax year runs from 6 April to the following 5 April.

Basis periods

Profits are taxed for the year to the accounting date in the *current* tax year. 30 April is a good accounting date to use as it gives the longest interval between earning profit and paying tax on it. However, the advantage is much less under the present 'Current Year Basis' (CYB) than under the old 'Previous Year Basis' (PYB) under which profits were taxed for the year to the accounting date in the *previous* year.

For example, for the tax year 1994/95 (which runs from 6 April 1994 to 5 April 1995), the basis period is:

- the year to 30 April 1993 under PYB, or
- the year to 30 April 1994 under CYB.

There were special rules for the opening and closing years of a business under PYB which provided considerable scope for tax planning. As these are no longer available to new businesses, they are not explained in this book.

Opening years – CYB

The profits in the tax year in which the business starts are assessed on an 'actual' basis – the taxable profit is the adjusted profit from when you start to the next 5 April. The second tax year is taxed on CYB, if there is a full year, or on the first year's trading if not. The third and subsequent years are taxed on CYB until the year of cessation.

Suppose a business starts on 1 June 1994 and uses 30 April as its accounting date. It will be taxed on these profits:

Tax year	*Basis period*
1994/95	1 June 1994 to 5 April 1995 (actual)
1995/96	1 June 1994 to 31 May 1995 (first year's trading)
1996/97	1 May 1995 to 30 April 1996 (CYB)

From this, it can be seen that there are two periods whose profits are taxed twice, namely from 1 June 1994 to 5 April 1995 and 1 May 1995 to 31 May 1995. These are known as the overlap period. Relief for this is given when the business ceases.

Closing year – CYB
In the tax year that the business closes, its basis runs from the end of the last basis period used to the close of the business. From this amount is deducted the taxable profits for the overlap period.

For example, our business above ends on 30 September 2003.

Its last full tax year was 2002/03. For that tax year it was taxed on its profits for the basis period to 30 April 2002.

For the tax year 2003/04, it is taxed from the end of that basis period to the date of cessation, namely for the period 1 May 2002 to 30 September 2003. In other words, for its final six months of existence, it is taxed on 17 months' profits. But from this amount it may claim overlap relief. This means it can deduct the amount of profit taxed twice in the opening years. In our example, this is the ten months from June 1994 to April 1995, and the one month of May 1995. With overlap relief, the business is taxed on six months' profit in the last six months of its life. Thus all profits earned throughout the life of the business are taxed once and once only (unlike PYB).

There are special provisions if the business changes its accounting date.

Transitional period – 1996/97 (historical interest)
A business which existed on 5 April 1994 is taxed on PYB for all

tax years up to 1995/96, and from CYB for tax years 1997/98. For the 1996/97 tax year, a business was taxed on the average of its profits for the two years covered using both PYB and CYB.

For example, a business established in 1983 uses 30 April as its accounting date. It will be taxed on these basis periods.

Tax year	Basis periods
1994/95	Year to 30 April 1993 (PYB)
1995/96	Year to 30 April 1994 (PYB)
1996/97	Average of year to 30 April 1995 (PYB) and year to 30 April 1996 (CYB)
1997/98	Year to 30 April 1997 (CYB)

Note what happens in tax year 1996/97. An average of two years' profits is taxed. The average of two numbers is half of one number plus half of the other. So another way of saying that the average of two years' profits is taxed is to say that for two years, you are only taxed on half your profits.

For example, the business above has profits for these years:

Accounting year to	Taxable profit
30 April 1994	£100,000
30 April 1995	£120,000
30 April 1996	£150,000
30 April 1997	£200,000
total for four years	£570,000

Under the transitional rules, it will be taxed on these amounts:

Tax year	Taxable profits in basis period
1995/96	£100,000
1996/97	£135,000
1997/98	£200,000
total for three years	£435,000

You will notice that only £435,000 has been taxed out of £570,000 profit. This is a rough part-compensation for the fact that when the business started, some of its profits in the early years were taxed two or three times under PYB.

Transitional overlap

Overlap relief is also claimable by businesses trading before 6 April 1994.

For the accounting period straddling 5 April 1997, some of the assessment falling within 1996/97 will be taxed in 1997/98. It is intended that the profits for this period will be relieved in the final tax year of the business.

In the example above the overlap period is from 1 May 1996 to 5 April 1997, 11/12 of the year. So 11/12 of the profit of £140,000, which is £128,333, is overlap relief to be offset in the tax year of cessation.

This is the other part of the compensation for the double and treble taxation of the early years under PYB.

Reliefs

There are four types of relief which may be claimed:

• loss relief
• group relief and consortium relief (companies only)
• top-slicing relief
• double taxation relief.

If you make a loss in a business, you may offset that loss:

• against other income made in the current tax year
• against other income in the following tax year, provided you continue the business in that year
• against income from the same business in future years. This may be carried forward indefinitely.

A loss incurred in any of the first four years may be offset against all income of the three previous tax years, starting with the earliest. A loss incurred in the last tax year may be offset against all income of the three previous tax years. The choice of which loss relief to use is yours.

Group relief applies when one company owns more than half of another. A consortium exists when 75 per cent of its equity is owned by other companies, each of which owns 5 per cent. These reliefs allow losses to be passed between companies, with certain restrictions. These reliefs are unlikely to be of use to a small business.

Top-slicing relief allows large payments received in one year to be spread over two or more tax years. This avoids a person having tax at a higher rate because of an exceptional payment in one year. If it relates to copyright (such as when a musical work is first recorded), it can be spread over two or three years depending on how long it took to create. The sale of patent rights is spread over six years.

Double taxation relief applies when the same income falls to be taxed in two countries. Under a series of agreements reached between the UK government and the governments of other countries, your total tax is limited to the rate charged in the higher taxed country. So if you are liable to tax at 40 per cent in the UK and at 27 per cent in the USA, you will only pay 40 per cent tax. The UK and USA governments have an agreement to share the tax between them. This principle applies even for those countries where the UK does not have an agreement.

Annual payments
The commonest forms of allowable annual payments are:

* deeds of covenant
* mortgage interest and
* medical expense insurance for someone over 60.

These are deductible from your *total* taxable income, not just your Schedule D Case I or II income.

Deeds of covenant are now only effective in transferring money to charity. The charity claims back your tax. It makes no difference to your tax liability. Similarly, mortgage interest relief and medical insurance for the elderly are given at source at basic rate. Higher rate taxpayers may claim further tax relief for medical expenses for the elderly.

Mortgage interest relief is restricted to 10 per cent tax relief from 6 April 1998 (formerly 15 per cent, from 6 April 1995). Medical insurance for the elderly is restricted to 25 per cent tax relief from 6 April 1994.

Personal allowance
You are entitled to deduct a personal allowance from whatever figure you have now arrived at. The basic single personal allowance is £4,195 from 6 April 1998. A married couple also have an allowance of £1,900 at a rate of 15 per cent from 6 April 1998 (10 per cent from 6 April 1999). They may share this between them as they wish. The wife may claim up to half without her husband's consent. She needs her husband's agreement to claim more. If no claim is made, the allowance is given to the husband. An additional personal allowance of £1,900 may be claimed by:

• a married man with an incapacitated wife or
• a single person

if, in either case, they have custody of a child.

A taxpayer who is over 65 may be able to claim an age allowance instead of the personal allowance. The basic age allowance is:

• single taxpayer 75+: £5.600
• single taxpayer 65+: £5,410

If the taxpayer is married, a higher married couple's allowance also applies according to the age of the older partner:

• a partner 75+: £3,345
• a partner 65+: £3,305

This allowance is reduced by £1 for every £2 by which the taxpayer's income exceeds £16,200, until the basic personal allowance (with married couple's allowance, if married) is reached. For example, a man aged 70 has a wife aged 75. His income is £17,000. His basic allowance is £5,410 plus £3,345 higher married couple's allowance.

This equals £8,755. However, because his income of £17,000 is more than £16,200, half the £800 excess is deducted. So the allowance is reduced by £400 to £8,355. This is more than the amounts for a person under 65 of £4,195 + £1,900 = £6,095.

The married couple's allowance, additional personal allowance, married age allowances and widow's bereavement allowance are restricted to 15 per cent from 6 April 1995 and 10 per cent from 6 April 1999.

A taxpayer who is blind may claim another £1,330. A widow may claim £1,900 in the tax year of her bereavement and in the following year, provided she remains unmarried (a widower cannot claim for the subsequent year).

Tax rates
The rates of tax for 1998/99 are:

Income band	Tax rate	Cumulative tax
£0 - £4,300	20 per cent	£860
£4,301 - £27,100	23 per cent	£6,104
over £27,100	40 per cent	

Corporation tax

Introduction
Corporation tax is assessed on broadly the same basis as income tax, though with different rates and payment dates. The most significant changes otherwise are:

- capital gains of companies are subject to corporation tax, not capital gains tax
- there are no personal allowances
- loss relief cannot be claimed by carrying back from the opening year

Rate of tax
The first £300,000 of adjusted profit is taxed at 21 per cent. If the

profits exceed £1,500,000, they are taxed at 31 per cent. Profits between £300,000 and £1,500,000 are taxed at 24 per cent on the first £300,000 and at 33.5 per cent on the excess. Advance corporation tax (ACT) is paid on one-quarter of the amount of the dividend. ACT is abolished from April 1999.

When paid
A company is liable to pay corporation tax nine months after its year-end. There is no previous year basis, and no elections for years to be assessed on an actual basis. For accounting periods ending after 30 September 1993, corporation tax is paid under a system known as Pay and File. Companies assess their own corporation tax liability and pay it nine months after their year-end as now. They must submit their returns 12 months after the year-end. Group relief and capital allowances are claimed in the filed return. A system of self-assessment is being introduced from April 1999.

Administration

Both income tax and corporation tax are assessed according to information given in tax returns. For individuals from the tax year 1996/97 they 'self' assess and pay the tax due. This is paid in three tranches: the first two (based on the previous year's liability) on 31 January in the tax year and 31 July following, and a balancing payment ten months after the end of the tax year on the following 31 January. An initial penalty of £100 is payable for missing the filing date.

A tax appeal must be made within 30 days of the assessment by writing to the tax inspector who issued the assessment outlining the reason. The commonest reason is that the assessment is 'estimated and excessive'. The matter is then negotiated with the inspector and a settlement usually reached. If not, an appeal lies first to commissioners (tax magistrates) and then to the courts.

If the tax is paid late, interest is charged. The interest is not tax-deductible. Similarly if you are overcharged tax and wait before receiving repayment, you may receive interest known as a repayment supplement. There are penalties starting from £300 for delay in submitting a tax return (thankfully, this is rarely imposed in practice – but don't rely on that). For serious fraud, there are unlimited fines and imprisonment.

These administrative arrangements change on 6 April 1996.

10 National insurance

Introduction

National insurance started as a compulsory insurance policy against unemployment and other social security provision. Over the 50 years since its introduction in its present form, it has gradually evolved into a second income tax.

There are five classes of national insurance:

- class 1 is paid by employer and employee on the employee's earnings
- class 1A is paid by the employer only, on employees' company cars
- class 2 is paid by the self-employed
- class 3 is a voluntary contribution paid by an employee or self-employed person who otherwise has insufficient contributions
- class 4 which is paid by the self-employed

Although the self-employed pay two classes of national insurance (2 and 4) against one for employees (1), the amount thus collected is usually much less. The reason is that the self-employed have less entitlement to social security benefits. In particular, they cannot claim unemployment benefit from their contributions.

Rates

Class 2 national insurance is paid at a flat rate of £6.35 (from 6 April 1998) a week. It is usually paid by direct debit from your bank. If your earnings are less than £3,590, you may fill in a form CF10 (found in leaflet N127A, available from any social security office). This means that you are exempt from paying class 2 contributions. An application can only be backdated up to 13 weeks, so if you delay by more than three months in applying, you will be liable for some class 2 contributions.

Class 4 national insurance is paid at the rate of 6.0 per cent on profits between £7,310 and £25,220 a year. It is collected by Inland Revenue with your income tax.

The maximum amount of national insurance a self-employed person can pay is therefore:

- class 2: 53 x £6.35   = £336.55
- class 4: 6.0% x (£25,220 - £7,310) = £1,074.60
                                                  £1,411.15

Class 3 voluntary contributions are £6.25 a week.

Entitlement

Class 2 contributions entitle the self-employed to claim these social security benefits:

- retirement pension
- sickness benefit
- widow's payment, widow's allowance and widowed mother's allowance.

Employees paying class 1 contributions are entitled to all the above, plus:

- invalidity benefit and
- jobseeker's allowance.

In addition, only employees are entitled to statutory sick pay or statutory maternity pay. Only employees may contribute to SERPS, the state earnings-related pension scheme.

Other benefits, such as child benefit, attendance allowance, industrial death benefit and disability living allowance, do not depend on contributions. Similarly, benefits such as family credit and income support are means-tested and available to the self-employed.

It is not strictly true that the self-employed are excluded from jobseeker's allowance. The entitlement arises from paying class 1 national insurance in the two previous tax years. So if you were employed for two years to 5 April 1997, went self-employed on 6 April 1997 and gave up in, say, January 1998, you would still be entitled to jobseeker's allowance.

If your class 2 contributions are too low to count towards your benefits for that year, the Department of Social Security (DSS) will invite you to make voluntary class 3 contributions. These count for the same benefits as class 2. It is usually advisable to make the class 3 contributions. Only complete years of contributions count towards the state retirement benefit.

Class 4 contributions do not count towards any benefits.

11 Value added tax

Introduction

Value added tax is charged on supplies of goods and services made in the course of a business. It may only be charged by those who have registered for VAT. The tax is charged at a standard rate or at a zero-rate unless the supply is exempt. VAT is administered by HM Customs & Excise to whom returns are made. The returns are usually made quarterly, though they can be made monthly or annually.

The following is a brief summary of VAT provisions likely to be of most relevance to a small business. It is essential to read and understand the VAT Guide provided free when you register, and to understand any provisions specifically relevant to your business. If you are in the construction industry, set aside at least an afternoon and have a bottle of Scotch handy.

Registration

Every Budget a VAT registration threshold is set. The threshold applicable from 1 April 1998 is £50,000. You *must* register for VAT if your supplies:

- have exceeded that limit in the last 12 months or
- there is good reason to believe that the taxable supplies in the next 30 days will exceed the limit.

Registration must be sought within 30 days of the end of the month in which the requirement was met. The limit only applies to taxable supplies. The value of exempt supplies may be ignored. If your supplies are wholly or largely zero-rated, you may request to be excused registration. If your turnover is below the threshold, you *may* register voluntarily. If your turnover falls below another limit, currently £48,000, you may apply to be deregistered.

When you are registered, you are given a certificate with your number. This comprises nine digits in the form NNN NNNN NN. If your circumstances change, you must notify Customs within 30 days of the change.

The rates of VAT

Standard rate

The standard rate of VAT has been 17.5 per cent since 1 April 1991. All supplies of goods and services are standard-rated unless specifically zero-rated or exempt.

The tax is charged on your value added. If you buy materials for £400, you actually pay your supplier £470 (assuming he is registered). The extra £70 is 17.5 per cent of £400. Suppose you then sell the item for £600, possibly after working on it. You actually charge your customer £705. The extra £105 is 17.5 per cent of £600. If your purchase and sale were in the same quarter, you would pay £105 (output tax) less £70 (input tax) which equals £35. This is 17.5 per cent of the £200 value added by you.

All the time supplies are made from one VAT-registered trader to another, no trader is bearing any VAT. The supplier charges us £70 VAT which we simply deduct from our next payment. The VAT is finally borne by the end-user, but Customs have received that VAT in instalments at every stage in the value added process.

Note that if you are quoted a price which includes VAT, the VAT element is not 17.5 per cent of the total, but 7/47 (which is 14.894 per cent). Also note that you cannot claim input tax on a car or on any non-business purchases.

Zero-rating and exemption

If an item is zero-rated, it bears VAT at a rate of 0 per cent. If it is exempt, it does not bear VAT at all. The difference between the two is that you can generally claim back VAT you have paid (input tax) for zero-rated supplies you make, but not for exempt supplies. If all your supplies are exempt, you cannot claim back input tax at all. If some supplies you make are exempt, your input tax is restricted to the share of output which is standard-rated or zero-rated. For example, if your supplies are equally divided between standard-rated, zero-rated and exempt, you may claim back two-thirds of your input tax. This is known as partial exemption.

If your exempt input tax is low, you may be able to avoid partial exemption and claim back all your input tax. From 1 December 1994 an additional criterion was introduced which needs to be satisfied. VAT incurred on the exempt supplies must be no more than 50 per cent of the VAT on all purchases. The limit of exempt tax is on average £625 a month. However, certain financial services are always regarded as partially exempt.

Zero-rating

The following items are zero-rated:

• food
• water and sewerage services to non-commercial premises
• books, magazines etc
• talking books for the blind
• news services
• construction of new non-commercial premises
• certain works on listed buildings
• international services
• public transport
• caravans and houseboats
• gold
• bank notes
• drugs, medicines and aids for the handicapped
• exports
• tax-free shops

- certain charitable supplies
- children's clothing and protective helmets and boots.

Exempt supplies

- land
- insurance
- postal services
- betting, gaming and lotteries
- finance
- health
- education
- burial and cremation
- trade unions and professional bodies
- sports competitions and
- works of art
- fund-raising events by charities, etc.

Exact scope

Please note that the above only gives the general scope of those items which are zero-rated or exempt. It is essential to get a detailed list from the appropriate VAT booklet (of which there are more than 100). They are famous for their detail. For example:

- baby shawls are zero-rated provided their sides are between 42 and 52 inches and they are white or a pastel shade of blue, pink or yellow
- dried fruit is zero-rated except banana chips which are standard-rated
- cherry trees are zero-rated except flowering cherry trees which are standard-rated
- Jaffa cakes, while looking like chocolate biscuits (Vatable) are deemed to be cakes (zero-rated).

Special provisions

Cash accounting

Generally, you must pay output tax when you have invoiced your customer and may deduct input tax when you have accepted an invoice from a supplier. When you pay or are paid is not relevant. If a customer does not pay you at all, you can generally reclaim the output tax when the debt is a year old and you have written it off.

However, if your turnover is less than £300,000, you may use cash accounting (see below). This means that you pay VAT only when you are paid. This has considerable cashflow advantages for most businesses. If you are never paid by a customer, you never pay the VAT on his supply.

You may continue using cash accounting until your turnover exceeds £375,000 a year.

Retail schemes

If you run a retail business, you may use one of the retail schemes. These schemes simplify the procedure for calculating your VAT, and may also save you VAT. For example, Scheme C assumes that fishmongers mark up their fish by 20 per cent and therefore requires VAT to be paid on one-sixth of retail sales of fish. It may be operated by a retailer with annual turnover up to £125,000. If you have a bigger mark-up on your fish, you will save VAT by using this scheme.

Obtain a copy of free VAT notice 727 which explains it all.

Second-hand goods

From 1 January 1995 the following applies to all second-hand goods. VAT is only assessed on the profit element when the goods are sold, provided certain records are kept.

Self-supply

If you are partly exempt and supply yourself with cars, stationery, construction services or building land, you must account for output tax on the value of the supply.

Annual accounting

If your turnover is less than £300,000, you may apply for annual accounting. It requires the approval of Customs and Excise. Broadly, you make one annual return of VAT two months after the year end. In the last nine months of the year you make equal payments equal to 90 per cent of the estimated VAT payable.

Monthly accounting

As an alternative to the normal quarterly returns, you may elect to make monthly returns. If your supplies are zero-rated but you have substantial standard-rated inputs, this can have considerable cashflow advantages.

Penalties

Introduction

The general law that you only pay a penalty if you have deliberately done something wrong does not apply for VAT. There are 15 different VAT penalties covering every trivial oversight imaginable. The penalties can be very severe and have attracted much criticism. The draconian serious misdeclaration penalty has had to be watered down three times in consecutive Budgets. It is still too harsh. On average, every VAT registered trader pays about £50 a year in penalties.

Customs and Excise are used to dealing with smugglers and moonshiners. They have not learned a more suitable approach for when Doris is confused over her wool shop's VAT return. Whereas Inland Revenue will be reasonable about imposing penalties, Customs automatically impose any penalty which the letter of the law allows. They once imposed a default surcharge for late submission of a VAT return on a trader whom they knew was unconscious with both arms in plaster.

For all penalties there is a defence of 'reasonable excuse'. Customs basically do not accept anything as a reasonable excuse. Fortunately, there is a cheap and simple appeal procedure to a VAT tribunal which tends to be more reasonable. It should also be said that Customs are notoriously inefficient in meeting the standards they expect others to follow. For example, the author asked for a form to be sent. It arrived five and a half months later with a notice saying that if not completed within 30 days, I was liable to a fine of £50.

The worst penalties
The three worst penalties are:

- failure to register
- late submission of return
- serious misdeclaration.

Failure to register for VAT attracts a penalty of up to 15 per cent of the tax you should have paid over, even though there may be no loss of tax through your non-payment. There is a minimum of £50.

The default surcharge is imposed at rates of up to 15 per cent of the tax involved. It is imposed for a second late payment or submission within any 12-month period. It starts at 2 per cent of the tax involved, and increases in steps for each subsequent default up to 15 per cent. There is a minimum penalty of £30.

The serious misdeclaration penalty is 15 per cent of the underdeclared tax, if the underdeclaration is more than any of:

- 30 per cent of the tax due
- £10,000 or
- 5 per cent of the tax due if it is more than £200,000.

In addition to the penalties, you are still liable to tax plus interest.

If you get caught for a large penalty and have even the slightest scrap of a good reason, it can be worth making an appeal to a VAT tribunal. If you find you have made a mistake, declare it immediately. That will reduce or even avoid the penalties. If you have any queries, contact your local VAT office for a ruling. Note the name of the person who gave it and exactly what he or she said. If the office is wrong (which is fairly common), it may be a good defence.

12 Other taxes

Summary

While income tax, corporation tax, national insurance and VAT are the most relevant taxes, there are others, namely:

- capital gains tax
- inheritance tax
- stamp duty
- customs duties
- excise duties and
- car tax.

Capital gains tax

Introduction

Capital gains tax (CGT) is charged on the profit made when a fixed asset is sold by an individual or partnership. Companies pay corporation tax on capital gains (where they are called 'chargeable gains'). The rules for eligibility and relief are the same for companies as for individuals, except that companies do not receive an annual exemption. CGT is alternative to income tax. If CGT is charged on a gain, income tax is not.

Scope

For CGT to be payable, three conditions must be met:

- a taxable person, must make

- a taxable supply of
- a taxable asset.

A taxable person is almost any person who is resident in the UK and not specifically exempted. Exemptions apply to charities, trade unions, local authorities, superannuation schemes, among others.

A taxable supply is a sale, loss, gift or other disposal other than:

- transactions between husband and wife
- gifts for the public benefit
- damages or compensation
- works of art
- terminations of a settlement,

among others.

A taxable asset is any asset other than:

- wasting assets – any asset with an expected life of less than 50 years, including all animals and vehicles
- payments from a superannuation fund
- insurance policies
- shares held under the Business Expansion Scheme
- foreign currency acquired for personal use
- private residence of the taxpayer
- qualifying corporate bonds and all government securities
- most settlements

among others.

Reliefs
The following reliefs are given:

- pre-1982 exemption
- indexation (up to April 1998)
- chattels relief
- annual exemption
- retirement relief (phased out from April 1999)

- holdover reliefs
- rollover reliefs and
- loss relief.

Any gain which arose before 6 April 1982 is excluded from CGT completely. Indexation removes from the gain the element which is due to general inflation as measured by the retail prices index. The indexation allowance is frozen from April 1998. Assets owned prior to that date and disposed of subsequently can claim the appropriate proportion from the date of purchase to April 1998. Indexation cannot increase a loss nor turn a gain into a loss.

Chattels are tangible movable property, basically anything you can see which is not fixed to a building. If chattels are disposed of for less than £6,000, they are exempt from CGT. If they are disposed of for more, the gain is limited to the lower of excess of the indexed gain, and five-thirds of the amount above £6,000.

An individual is entitled to an annual exemption. This is currently (from 6 April 1998) £6,800. If the gains, after indexation and all other reliefs and exemptions have been claimed, come to less than this figure, no CGT is payable. If they come to more, only the excess is taxable.

Retirement relief exempts business assets when the taxpayer either:

- reaches the age of 50 (from 28 November 1995) (whether he retires or not) or
- retires before reaching 50 because of ill health.

This is to be phased out over 5 years from April 1999. It is to be replaced from that date by a general tapering relief which reduces the tax charge for the longer the asset was held (max 10 years). There are differential tapers for business and non-business assets.

If the business assets do not exceed £250,000, they are completely exempt. If they exceed £250,000, half the excess to £1m is also exempted. The relief is only given in full if the assets have been owned for ten years. If they have been owned for a shorter period, the relief is proportionately reduced. So if a 60-year-old man disposes of £800,000 worth of business assets (after indexation etc.) which he has owned for eight years, he is limited to 8/10 of the full retirement relief which is £250,000 plus half of (£800,000 - £250,000). This works out at £425,000.

Holdover reliefs postpone a liability. They apply, broadly, when an asset is given away or transferred between connected people.

Rollover relief applies when a business asset is replaced, such as when a factory is sold and another bought. The relief postpones the CGT liability until the replacement is sold (unless that is also rolled over). The replacement must be acquired within 12 months before and three years after the disposal.

Loss relief allows capital losses to be offset against capital gains for the current year and future years indefinitely. In the year a taxpayer dies, the gains may be carried back to the three previous years. The loss relief is never claimed so that the annual exemption is lost. For example if you have capital gains in the current and next tax year each of £10,000 and loss relief of £8,000, you claim £3,200 this year to reduce your gain to £6,800 which is then exempted. The other £4,800 loss is carried forward to next year.

Rate
Capital gains tax is charged at the person's marginal rate of income tax as if it were an addition to their taxable income.

Inheritance tax

Scope
Inheritance tax is paid on money transferred on the death of a person or in the seven years before his death. The tax is usually paid by the estate of the deceased person.

Exemptions, reliefs and allowances
The exceptions and reliefs include:

• transfers between spouses

- an annual exemption for the estate of £3,000 a year while the testator was alive
- an annual exemption of £250 per donee per year
- gifts to charities, political parties and for public benefit
- quick success relief (when property passes on a second death within seven years of the first)
- taper relief (for transfers made between three and seven years before death)
- business property relief.

For deaths from 10 March 1992, the business property reliefs are:

- interests in unincorporated businesses (from 6 April 1996 of any size), in unquoted or USM companies, owner-occupied farmlands and farm tenancies: 100 per cent
- controlling holdings in fully quoted companies, assets owned by partners and used in the partnership: 50 per cent.

Rate
The first £223,000 (from 6 April 1998) of the assessable estate is exempt. The rest is taxable at 40 per cent.

Stamp duty

Stamp duty is a tax on documents, according to what the document does. Its scope has been considerably reduced this century. It is now charged on conveyance of land at a rate roughly equal to 1 per cent of the total value. On transactions below £60,000 no duty is payable; and on share transfers where the rate is usually 0.5 per cent of the value transferred. There are some small fixed duties which range from 25p to £2 per document.

Customs duties

Customs duties are paid on imported goods. The rates are very complex, according to an internationally agreed HS/TARIC numbering system of up to 15-digit numbers. The rates are published in *Customs & Excise Tariff* which has 21 sections.

In addition to these rates, the importer needs to consider any preferences or suspensions which may be in effect from that country. There are sometimes quotas negotiated by the EC with other countries, under which the duty is reduced. Sometimes an anti-dumping duty is imposed to thwart attempts by other countries (mostly Japan and Far Eastern countries) to destroy a home industry by 'dumping' imports at very low prices.

If importing regularly, it is worth familiarising yourself with this system. Otherwise a good shipping agent can advise.

Excise duties

Excise duties are taxes imposed on a small range of goods and services, notably:

- alcoholic drink
- tobacco products
- hydrocarbon oil (mostly petrol)
- betting and gaming.

There is also vehicle excise duty (VED), commonly known as road tax, as evidenced by discs on vehicles.

13 How to fiddle your tax

Introduction

Legality

Fiddling your tax is not illegal, providing you stay within the law. *Tax evasion* is the criminal offence of withholding or falsifying information. *Tax avoidance* is the legal arrangement of your affairs to minimise your tax liability. The matter was expressed almost poetically by this legal judgment in the case *Ayrshire Pullman Motor Services and Ritchies v Ritchies [1929]:* 'No man in this country is under the smallest obligation, moral or other, so to arrange his legal relations to his business or to his property as to enable the Inland Revenue to put the largest possible shovel into his stores. The Inland Revenue is not slow – and quite rightly – to take every advantage which is open to it under the taxing statutes for the purpose of depleting the taxpayer's pocket. And the taxpayer is, in like manner, entitled to be astute to prevent, so far as he honestly can, the depletion of his means by the Inland Revenue.'

If you do plan your tax within the law, you have nothing to hide. If the tax office ask why you have done something, you can simply say 'to avoid tax'. Inland Revenue is there to uphold the law. If the widow is taxed on her mite while the millionaire pays nothing, that is of no concern to Inland Revenue. Inland Revenue is neither a business nor a charity. It does not matter to them how much they collect from you. Do not take the view which is sometimes expressed as 'I pay the taxman something to keep him happy'. You should pay the correct amount, which may be zero. If you pay more, you are wasting your money. If you pay less, you commit an offence.

Objectives
The main objective is to reduce your tax liability within the law. This should be done within three criteria:

- the overall tax liability should be reduced. There is no point in saving income tax at 23 per cent only to pay more inheritance tax at 40 per cent
- the plan should be cost-effective. It is easy to spend £1,000 in fees to save £200 in tax
- the plan should not impose onerous conditions. If the scheme involves emigrating or giving property away, you need to consider whether you are prepared to accept those conditions.

Remember that tax laws change. Some people are stuck in elaborate capital transfer tax avoidance schemes – still avoiding a tax which was abolished in 1986. Other people turned investment income into capital gains in 1978 when the former was taxed at 98 per cent and the latter at 30 per cent. They are now taxed at the same rates. Some emigrated to Spain for sunshine and tax avoidance. They still have the sunshine, but Spain's tax rates are now much higher than the UK's.

Also remember that your circumstances change. You do not need to avoid a higher rate tax if you are no longer liable anyway. It is always advisable for any plan to be flexible, and, preferably, one that can be abandoned.

Artificiality
The leading marketing agency of tax avoidance schemes is the government. It encourages you to avoid tax through enterprise investment schemes, personal equity plans (PEPs), tax-exempt special savings accounts (TESSAs), profit-related pay, share option schemes, mortgage interest relief and the suchlike.

There are also well-worn paths of known tax avoidance schemes. Some of them have been in existence for nearly a century. Beware of straying from these well-worn paths into the thickets of artificial avoidance. Over one-tenth of the Income and Corporation Taxes Act 1988 is given to anti-avoidance provisions. Also some leading court cases of the 1980s established that a series of transactions whose only purpose is tax avoidance is ineffective. When tax rates are as low as 23 per cent, it may be better simply to pay tax rather than seek some clever avoidance scheme.

The following is by no means an exhaustive list of tax planning opportunities. They do however include most of the ones likely to be of use to a small business.

Accounting date (not companies)

The first plan is what accounting date to use. Both previous year basis and current year basis tax profits on the accounting year. So the earlier your accounting date in the tax year, the greater the period from when you earn the money to when you pay it. The tax year starts on 6 April. It is always convenient to have an accounting date which is the last day of a month, so 30 April is a common date.

When you start (not companies)

You may have no choice when to start your business. If you do, start as soon as possible *after* your accounting date. If you adopt 30 April, start your business in May.

Don't worry about any money you may have spent in advance in setting up your business. In your first year, you may claim any expenditure related to the business incurred in the previous seven years. So have a good think of anything which could be seen as pre-trading expenditure. You cannot claim anything for which you have already had tax relief.

If you were previously employed, there is a second advantage in starting in May. Your entitlement to the jobseeker's allowance depends on you having made class 1 national insurance contributions in the two previous tax years. If you start on 1 May, you have until the following 5 April, more than 11 months, to see if the business will work. It is a form of insurance policy. If it does not work, you can end it and claim the jobseeker's allowance. If you started your business on 1 March, you would only have five weeks.

Starting a second business (not companies)

One person may run more than one business. However, if there is any connection between the two, Inland Revenue may refuse to accept that these are two separate businesses. In the case *Scales v George Thompson & Co Ltd [1929]*, the judge said, 'the real question is, was there any inter-connection, any interlacing, any unity at all embracing those two businesses?'. A more recent test case was *Seaman v Tucketts Ltd [1956]*. A confectionery manufacturer which bought cellophane and sugar, stopped manufacture and sold the cellophane and sugar to a parent company for cost plus 10 per cent. This was held to be a new business.

In reality, it is not too difficult to establish that a new line is a separate business. However, you must keep separate books. If you give it a separate legal form, such as a sole trader running a second business as a partnership with his wife, it helps your case. Any other distinctions that can sensibly be made should be. For example, you may operate from separate premises, have a different accounting date and a different management policy.

An advantage of a second business is that you can use the benefits of opening basis periods again. If your new business makes a loss (which can easily be arranged), you can claim current loss relief against past profits. It is possible this way to make good profits while not paying any tax and carrying loss relief forward. When you start to get cluttered with new businesses, the next section explains how to get more tax advantage by shutting them down. The benefit is much reduced under the current year basis.

Employing your wife or husband (not companies)

A common ploy is to employ one's wife in the business. If she earns less than her personal allowance (and has no other income), she pays no tax on the money and you get the full tax relief. This means that you can pay her £4,195.

In reality, the figure is usually pitched just above or below the lower earnings limit for class 1 national insurance. This is currently

£3,328 a year. Just below this figure, you have the full tax relief without either you or her having to pay national insurance. However, you may consider it worth paying just above this figure so that your wife establishes her own national insurance record. For example, if you pay exactly £3,328, your wife will pay £66.56 national insurance in the year. As employer you would benefit from a low rate of 3 per cent meaning that you pay £99.84.

So for a total of £166.40 a year, your wife can establish her full entitlement to all national insurance benefits. For example if you 'sacked' her after two years' contributions, she would be entitled to a full year's jobseeker's allowance. At current rates that means she would receive £2,650 in a year for contributions of £332.80 – a good return. Of more importance, she would earn towards the full retirement pension, currently £64.70 a week, rather than a non-contributory pension of £38.70 a week based on the husband's contributions.

Even greater benefits can be achieved by using fringe benefits. This is because the benefits are generally only fully taxed when the person's income and benefits exceed £8,500 a year. For example, if the wife is given a salary of £3,328, she can also be given a new £10,000 1.5-litre car. The notional tax liability of the car is £3,500 plus £1,280 for the petrol (assuming she does fewer than 2,501 business miles). This totals £8,108 which is less than £8,500. So the wife pays no tax at all on the car (or any other element of her salary), while you can claim against your tax the full capital allowance for the car and all the petrol and other expenses of the car.

Since 1990, these plans work just as well when a wife employs her husband.

To make this arrangement work, it is essential that the money be paid to the husband or wife and that they do enough work to justify the payment. Answering the telephone, typing a few letters or entertaining clients can easily be good enough. It does not matter for tax purposes whether the husband or wife does more than enough to earn the amount. Inland Revenue is not part of the Low Pay Unit. Inland Revenue may question such an arrangement on the basis that the payment actually represents housekeeping and ask for details of your domestic arrangements. Tell them to mind their own business. The law requires a husband and wife to support each other financially.

How they do this is their business. If the husband and wife agree that she will earn her housekeeping in her husband's business, that is quite legal and no one else's concern.

Incorporation

The relative advantages of becoming a company rather than a sole trader are explained in chapter 2. Usually you incorporate when your personal tax exceeds the basic rate of income tax. However, this assumes a simple structure that you are either one thing or the other. In reality, it is possible to have a more complex structure whereby different aspects of your work may be effected by different means. It is possible to have a partnership and a company, or several companies. It is even possible for a company itself to be a partner.

Government-backed schemes

The government produces many schemes designed to avoid tax for you. Do not think that tax avoidance is only effective if it works against government policy. For the small business, the most effective tax avoidance scheme is a personal pension plan. Other schemes may offer similar tax advantages, but few will approach the return likely to be achieved by a personal pension. You can invest between 17.5 per cent and 40 per cent of your relevant income in a pension plan. Contributions may be carried back against the previous six years' income.

Elections

There are over 50 different elections which you can make in connection with tax. These include:

- loss relief may be relieved in several different ways
- the married couple's allowance may be freely transferred between husband and wife.

- adopting annual accounting, cash accounting or a special retail scheme for VAT.

Companies

If you run a company, you have a choice of taking funds out as dividend or salary. For a small business the income tax/corporation tax liability is likely to be the same whichever method is used. However, dividends have the advantage that national insurance is avoided.

If you are about to sell a capital asset for which holdover relief is not available for capital gains tax, it can be tax-effective to incorporate then as companies may in general offset capital losses against income.

No profits and capital allowances

Capital allowances are deductions from taxable profits. If you have no taxable profits, you do not receive any benefit. The allowance may be carried forward indefinitely, but can only be relieved against ultimate profits and losses because of inflation during that time.

An alternative is to lease the asset. Even if you have already bought the asset, it is a common procedure to sell the asset and lease it back. The lessor claims the capital allowance and passes some of the benefit to you through reduced lease rental.

Value added tax stagger periods

Generally, you have a choice of stagger periods. This is the quarterly date to which you must make your return. For convenience, let us assume that you have chosen the sequence 31 March, 30 June, 30 September and 31 December. If you have scope legitimately to manipulate the date of invoices, move the sales invoices to just after the stagger date and the purchase invoices to just before. Thus if you receive an invoice dated 31 March you can claim back the VAT on it immediately, even before you have paid the invoice. If you issue an invoice on 1 April, you do not have to account for the VAT on it until 31 July. Postponing it that one day gives you an extra three months' free credit. Obviously this does not apply if you are on the cash accounting scheme. The above example uses stagger '1'; quarters ending January, April, July and October are known as stagger '2'. Stagger '3' is for quarters ending February, May, August and November. To change your stagger telephone your VAT office.

If you control two VAT-registered businesses making taxable supplies, they can have different stagger dates. For example, A has a date of 31 March, B has 30 April. If A invoices B on 1 April, B can claim back the tax during April, but A does not have to pay it until 31 July. If B invoices A on 1 May, A can claim back the tax during July, but B does not have to pay it until August. The invoices between A and B must be for actual supplies. If you invent a non-existent supply you can be prosecuted by Customs. However, if one business pays the overheads such as telephone, heating, etc., an invoice for a management charge is a legitimate invoice.

Value added tax voluntary registration

If your income is below the level at which you must register for VAT, you have the choice of voluntarily registering. It is usually advisable to do so if:

• your customers are entirely or mostly VAT-registered and
• your supplies are entirely or almost entirely standard-rated.

The two advantages of registration under these circumstances are:

• you can claim back input tax on your purchases and
• Customs & Excise subsidise your cashflow.

For example, your monthly invoices are about £2,000. You spend £400 a month on standard-rated items (such as stationery and most raw materials). By registering for VAT, you will invoice at £2,350 a month. Your customer will pay you the extra £350 and deduct it from his VAT bill, so it has cost him nothing. That extra £350 will have to be paid over by you to Customs, so there is no permanent gain. However you have between one and four months' free use of the money. If the bank is charging you 13 per cent interest on your borrowings, this could save you £150 a year in interest charges.

Your standard-rated purchases of £400 a month include £59.58 of VAT. This you can now claim back. Over a year, this will save you £715 in VAT. The two advantages together save about £865.

Late payment

The interest on late tax is loosely linked to prevailing interest rates. The current rate of 9.5 per cent (from 6 August 1997) may appear attractive compared with perhaps 12 per cent charged by the bank. However, bank interest it tax-deductible whereas interest on late tax is not. If you owe £1,000 to Inland Revenue for a year, they will charge you £95 interest; the bank will charge you £120. However, you can claim tax relief on the bank interest. At 23 per cent, £120 reduces to £92.40; at 40 per cent it reduces to £72, making the bank interest cheaper.

Small businesses will be fortunate to be able to borrow at 12 per cent. If the rate charged by the bank is 15 per cent, the interest of £150 reduces to £115.50 for a basic rate taxpayer, still more than Inland Revenue charge. It can be cheaper to run up an interest charge with Inland Revenue than it is to increase your overdraft by paying the tax. Curiously, Inland Revenue are fully aware of this, but for years have done nothing about it. Whether it is worth running up the overdraft can be done by comparing interest rates. However, the Inland Revenue may not leave you alone for 12 months without seeking to collect monies due!

The rate charged by the bank is usually limited to the base rate at the time. The Inland Revenue interest rate is itself related to the base rate. Note that you must still submit your returns even if you are not paying the tax to avoid the penalties.

If you have sufficient funds to pay your VAT or your income tax, but not both, pay the VAT. Their penalties are more severe and they are stricter in enforcing them.

Dealing with tax authorities

Simply how you deal with the tax authorities can in itself save you money.

First of all, be prompt. A tax return takes just as long to complete tomorrow as it does today. But tomorrow you could be liable for penalties for being late. Remember that penalties are in addition to the interest you pay.

Claim all the expenses, allowances and other deductions to which you are entitled. Remember that for income tax, you can claim all expenditure which is wholly and exclusively used for your business. It does not have to be necessary. If you pay a subscription to a professional body, that subscription is probably tax-deductible.

Do not volunteer unnecessary information. If your turnover is less than £15,000, you only need submit three-line accounts: turnover, expenses and profits. Even if above, you do not have to provide much more detail. You simply analyse the income and expenses into a few appropriate categories. You should not identify your customers or suppliers in the accounts, nor submit copies of invoices and other documents. If Inland Revenue want to know who they are (unlikely in practice), let them ask.

Certain items will automatically be queried. These include 'entertainment' and 'legal fees'. Either disallow them yourself by adding them back in the tax computation, or explain in a note to the accounts why they are allowable. Better still, avoid the terms completely. Taking your staff to the pub after a long session is 'staff welfare'. Parking tickets are 'motoring expenses', and you can deduct them from your taxable profits.

Even though the law on allowable expenditure has remained mostly unchanged for over 100 years, there is still a surprisingly large grey area in what is allowable. If you have such a grey item, give yourself the benefit of any doubt, but disclose its nature in a note to the accounts. If you state the item clearly in the accounts and

Inland Revenue do not challenge it, you can become entitled to tax relief even if the law does not strictly allow it. The legal decision was established in the case *Scorer v Olin Energy Systems Ltd [1985]* and codified by Inland Revenue in their statement of practice SP8/91.

If Inland Revenue ask you a question, answer it. They do not have armies of people intercepting your post or spying on you through binoculars. You are probably their only source of information about you. However, if a letter says they believe 'your tax affairs may not be correct in all respects' (or similar), you are under investigation and should immediately get professional advice.

Always be civil to Inland Revenue staff. They are not allowed to be rude to you. It is unfair to be rude to them. Compared with social security staff and even Customs and Excise staff, Inland Revenue are very courteous and helpful. A gracious manner always commends you. As tax inspectors have wide discretion, coming over as someone who is honest and charming can only help your cause. Do not berate them with your opinions about government spending. If you must sound off about these matters, write to your MP or a newspaper.

You do not have to accept an inspector's decision. You then have 30 days in which to write to him, briefly outlining your reasons for appeal. It is usual at the same time to appeal for postponement of any tax which may be due. If the 30 days has expired, you can ask for permission to make a late appeal. It is generally given.

In reality, the matter can usually be resolved amicably by correspondence or a telephone call. If the matter lends itself to such treatment, you can always ask to meet the inspector. If, unusually, you believe the tax office is being unreasonable, you can write to the area office. If, also unusually, the matter cannot be resolved between you and the inspector, you have the right to appeal to commissioners. There are two types:

- general commissioners who are lay people, independent of Inland Revenue, and holding a similar position to magistrates
- special commissioners, who are specialists employed by Inland Revenue.

In many cases, you may choose who hears your appeal. If your argument involves nit-picking technicalities of tax law, choose the special commissioners. If your argument appeals to a sense of fairness as seen by the ordinary man, choose the general commissioners. The commissioners' decision is final on a point of fact. On a point of law, you may appeal further to the law courts. You have no reason to fear a commissioners' hearing. The meeting is held in private, there are no costs, and you may represent yourself or be represented by an accountant or solicitor.

Similarly, if you have a dispute with Customs over your VAT, you have nothing to fear from a VAT tribunal hearing. Although costs can be awarded, in practice they only are if you have been unreasonable in your behaviour. The fact that you lose does not in itself make you liable for any costs. Customs are fond of imposing penalties willy-nilly and disregarding any 'reasonable excuse'. The tribunals are generally more reasonable and frequently set penalties aside.

14 Pensions

The need

Quickly calculate the amount you need for your day-to-day living expenses. Compare that with £64.70 a week (£103.40 if you are married). That is what you will have to live on if you rely only on the state pension.

If you have been employed, you may have 'frozen' or 'deferred' pensions from your employers. They may pay your milk bill. Before 1988, occupational pension schemes were legalised protection rackets as far as early leavers were concerned. Even if you did not have the misfortune to work for a company run by Robert Maxwell, your contributions either accrued no benefit, or accrued at a lower rate than if you have stayed at the company. If you have such schemes, don't get too excited. The pension they give may *not* pay your milk bill.

In contrast, a personal pension can provide a much larger chunk of income. However optimistic you are about being a millionaire at 65, take out a personal pension. Although you can provide for your future by ordinary saving, a personal pension has two great advantages:

- it enjoys considerable tax relief and
- it removes the uncertainty of your life expectancy.

Pension funds enjoy three tax concessions over other forms of saving:

- your contributions are tax-deductible
- the income earned by the fund is tax-free (dividends are taxed)
- the lump sum from the fund is tax-free

The uncertainty is that you never know how long you have left to live. At 65, a British man has, on average, 13 years to live. A woman has 17 years. However, there is a one in five chance he will live for 20 years (to 85), and a one in 500 chance that he will live to 100. You need a large amount of capital for a small income. To provide £10,000 a year income, you need about £100,000 in investments. To allow for inflation during your retirement years, you must spend about half the interest. That means you would need £200,000 in investments. And could you live on the state pension plus £10,000 a year anyway?

The tax advantages of a pension over, say, a building society account make pensions much more attractive over time. If the rates at which they earn interest are the same, a pension can earn half as much again as the building society over five years. Over ten years, it earns more than double. And you may have 30 years before you retire.

The certainty is that you receive a known amount each year, regardless of how long you live. You may have more than one pension plan.

Outline of how a pension scheme works

The two stages
In a pension scheme, money is put into a fund (the 'pot') where it grows with interest until you decide to retire. This money is then used to buy an annuity. This is an arrangement whereby an insurance company accepts a lump sum in return for providing an agreed amount each year. This is based on how long they expect you to live. Those who die young in effect subsidise those who live long.

A pension scheme therefore has two separate stages:

• building up the fund and
• buying the annuity.

These are two stages which can be implemented quite independently. There is no reason why the company which builds up the fund should also sell you the annuity that actually provides you with the pension. If the stages can be applied independently, the scheme is said to have an 'open market option'. The fund should build up to a substantial amount. A figure of £200,000 is not excessive.

Usually you must take the pension between the ages of 50 and 75. The later you retire, the higher the pension you receive. The increase can be very significant because there are two factors which are increasing the amount:

- you make more contributions and earn more interest, so the pot is larger and
- you have fewer years to live in which the pension is paid.

If you took out the pension to contract out of the state scheme, SERPS, the government may be paying another 1 per cent of your contributions as 'incentive bonus'. The figure was 2 per cent before 6 April 1992.

What happens at retirement
When you retire, you can receive some of the money as a tax-free lump sum. Generally, this is around a quarter of the fund. So if your fund has built up to £200,000, you can receive up to £50,000 as a tax-free lump sum. You do not have to take any lump sum, or can choose to take a smaller sum. However, you only have the one chance to take it.

The rest of the fund is used to buy an annuity. The amount it buys depends on your age, your sex and the state of the annuity market at the time. The following gives an idea of typical current rates of how much each £1,000 of fund will buy each year:

- man aged 60: £107
- man aged 65: £117
- man aged 70: £130
- woman aged 55: £90
- woman aged 50: £97
- woman aged 65: £104

So with a £200,000 fund, a 65-year-old man may have a pension of 200 x £117 = £23,400 a year, and no lump sum. Or he may take a tax-free lump sum of £50,000, and have an annual pension of 150 x £117 = £17,550.

It must be stressed that these are typical figures based on current rates under current law. The actual amount you receive depends on the rates prevailing at that time, how well your fund performs and what the law is. The law has changed radically many times during the 1980s. Pensions have also become a football between the political parties, though all parties agree the need for pensions in principle.

Your normal pension is subject to income tax in the same way as earnings as an employee. However, as the amount is less, it is more likely that you will be paying at basic rate and will avoid higher rate liabilities. Tax is usually deducted at source under PAYE. You do not pay national insurance on pension receipts.

Other benefits

You have certain options other than just lump sum and regular pension. Usually you exercise the option at retirement. The options are summarised below.

- *Index-linking* increases the pension, to contribute towards inflation. As a rough guide, to receive a pension which fully reflects inflation, you start with a figure about half of what you would otherwise receive.
- *Pension guarantee* means that you are guaranteed your pension for a minimum time, often five years. This means that if you die one year after starting your pension, your family will receive another four years' worth.
- *Wife and children* may be entitled to receive a pension if they survive you. A husband or wife is limited to two-thirds of what you would receive. Your dependent children are together limited to two-thirds of what your husband or wife would receive, which is four-ninths of what you would receive.

All the above items must be 'bought' from the fund when you retire. Before then you may 'buy':

- *Illness cover.* If you become unable to work, this extra premium will allow you to stop making further payments, but still continue your full pension entitlement. It is in effect a form of life insurance.

If you die before reaching retirement age, your estate will receive a refund of your contributions with some interest.

Other provisions

State pension

Provided you have paid *sufficient* national insurance contributions, you will receive the basic state retirement pension from the age 65 (men) or 60 (women). The government is required to equalise these ages. This is to become 65 for both sexes. There is to be a phasing-in period commencing in 2010. The later they leave it, the higher their pension will be. There is already in effect a five-year period, as you can defer the pension to receive a higher amount. Each week you defer it, your pension increases by 1/7 of 1 per cent. If you defer your pension for the full five years, it increases by just over 37 per cent.

If you have paid insufficient national insurance contributions for the state retirement pension, you are entitled to a non-contributory pension from the age of 80. The retirement pension (from 6 April 1998) is £64.70 for a single person; £103.40 for a married couple; and £38.95 for someone who has paid no contributions and is 80. All pensions increase by 25p a week from the age of 80. If the current pension is fully deferred, it becomes £88.96 (single) or £142.16 (married).

If you are unclear about your current pension entitlements there is a form obtainable from the local Social Security office – form BR19 (Retirements Pensions Forecast Form) – which will enable you to apply for a full analysis of your current expectations.

SERPS

If you have been an employee since 1978, you will probably have paid contributions into the State Earnings Related Pension Scheme (SERPS). The self-employed cannot join SERPS, but may keep an entitlement already built up.

To find out how much entitlement you may have under SERPS, you can ask for a form NP38 available from any social security office. This form is completed and posted or handed in at the social security office. The department will (eventually) write advising of your entitlement. This service is free.

Graduated pension

If you were an employee between April 1961 and April 1975, you will probably have paid a graduated contribution to a pre-SERPS state scheme. Under this scheme you bought units which entitle you to a weekly pension. The rate of pension per unit bought increases each year. For 1998/99 the rate is 8.4p per unit (8.6p in 1999/00), so that if a man had 86 units (the maximum possible) he would receive a graduated weekly pension of 86 x 8.4p = £7.22. A woman's maximum is 48 units.

Occupational pension schemes

If you were in a company pension scheme for less than two years, you will probably have received a refund of contributions when you left.

If you were in a scheme for a longer period, you will probably be entitled to a deferred pension. That means that when you retire, you must try to track down the company or its fund and claim your pension. The rules on deferred pensions are very complicated and have been changed many times. At its simplest, contributions made since 1 January 1985 are increased by at least 5 per cent each year. Contributions before are probably not increased at all. Those still in the company scheme are benefiting at your expense.

If you make additional voluntary contributions (AVCs), the treatment depends on whether they were 'in house' or 'free-standing'. In house AVCs increase your deferred entitlement. Free-standing AVCs can be taken by you when you leave. They are, in effect, a separate pension plan.

The exact details are available from the scheme's trustees. They should have given you the information when you left. If not, ask them for details.

Retirement annuities
Retirement annuities were similar to personal pension plans, though less flexible. No new policies have been written since 1 July 1988, but existing policies may continue.

Limits

There are no limits on the number of pension plans you may have, nor on the amount you may pay into them. However, there are limits on the amount you may contribute and get tax relief. The limit is a percentage of 'net relevant earnings' (broadly, your taxable income). It depends on your age at the beginning of the tax year.

Age	Limit
to 35	17.5%
36–45	20%
46–50	25%
51–55	30%
56–60	35%
over 60	40%

If your contributions exceed this percentage, you can offset the excess against your income for the previous six years, or carry it forward against future income indefinitely.

Choosing a scheme

Schemes are marketed by insurance companies. There are specialist magazines which review how well the schemes perform.

You can always seek advice from a financial intermediary. Remember that intermediaries are either 'tied', which means that they may only recommend one company's products, or 'free' which means that they may recommend any product. They choose the ones with the biggest commission. You can be better advised asking your accountant to whisper a name in your ear.

If looking at tables, choose one which has consistently come near the top. Every rep will have tables showing how his company does just that. If you have to talk to a financial intermediary, try these questions (and act a bit daft).

- *What is the investment return?*
  The correct answer is 'I don't know', but he should be able to show you tables of past achievement. Ignore tables which show growth according to standard LAUTRO rules. He is not selling you the idea of having a personal pension. You should already be sold on that. He is selling his scheme.

- *Does the pension offer the open market option?*
  The answer should be yes. This means that the annuity does not have to be provided by the company that built up the fund.

- *What happens if I die before retirement age?*
  They must all refund your contributions. Better funds will give you the accumulated fund.

- *Is there a guaranteed benefit if I die soon after retirement?*
  The answer should be yes.

- *What will my policy be worth in five years' time?*
  This is a crafty way of asking what the charges are. If the charges are high, the fund will not have recovered within five years.

- *Can I decrease or increase my contributions without extra charge or penalty?*
  You need this flexibility for changed circumstances. There is no reason why the scheme should not offer it.

15 Insurance

Introduction

Insurance is often resented in the small business. It is yet another area where money goes out and nothing comes in. Insurance is cheap the first time you use it. If something is worth insuring, it usually means that you cannot carry on in business without it.

There are many different policies which a business may need. In practice, insurance companies often offer one policy which covers all the items required. If you work from home or use your car for work, you should check your insurance policies to see whether you are covered for work. Having taken out your insurance, make sure the policies are reviewed each year.

Premises

The premises you use must be insured, whether they are owned freehold, leasehold or are leased. You do not have to insure the land. You must insure the buildings for the cost of rebuilding, which is usually more than the cost of buying another building. This cost includes architect's fees and site clearance costs. It also includes providing you with temporary accommodation.

Do not be tempted to under-insure. For example, if you own three shops each of which should be insured for £180,000, it may be tempting to insure all three for £180,000 on the grounds that it is most unlikely that they would burn down on the same day. This will not work. The insurance company will apply 'averaging', and only pay you £60,000 for each shop.

Equipment and stock

Equipment must be insured for its replacement value. If a new lathe costs £10,000, that is what it must be insured for. What the lathe is worth second-hand or shown as in your books is irrelevant. Insurance is to get you going again. If you lose your lathe, the proceeds must buy you a new one. The replacement value of equipment tends to be much higher than you think.

Leased equipment must be insured by you, noting the lessor's interest. For plant and machinery, it may be necessary to insure against the consequences of breakdown. Office equipment is usually insured separately from plant and machinery. Stock is normally valued at its cost as this is usually its replacement value. Note that stock cannot readily be insured against shoplifting and staff theft.

Business interruption

If your factory burns down or all your stock is lost, you not only need to replace it, you need compensation for the business lost while you were replacing it. If your profits are £2,000 a week, and a serious catastrophe could stop you for six weeks, you need business interruption insurance of £12,000.

Employer's liability

It is a legal requirement that employers insure their staff against death, bodily risk or disease sustained while at work. The law is Employers' Liability (Compulsory Insurance) Act 1969. The certificate must be conspicuously displayed on the premises.

Public liability

Any person who suffers death, injury or disease because of your business or because of your premises may claim against you. The fact that you were not negligent in any way does not excuse you from liability. Although the chances are remote, the damages can now run into millions of pounds.

Cars

Drivers must be insured before they use British roads. Ordinary domestic car insurance policies do not always cover business use. This can often be added to your insurance policy for little or no extra premium. An employer is vicariously liable for injury caused by an employee driving on business. If your van driver injures or kills someone or damages another vehicle or property, you are liable. This needs to be covered in the insurance.

Commercial vehicles

Commercial vehicles are insured under special policies. For example, policies for vehicles carrying loads often include insurance for loss while loading and unloading. Commercial vehicles are classified according to whether they carry goods, carry people, are for agriculture or forestry, or for a special purpose. There are also special policies for ships and aircraft.

Book debts

There is limited scope for insuring debts against non-payment. This is often done in conjunction with a debt factoring or discounting service. Export debts are usually insured through Export Credit Guarantee Department (ECGD). They can be contacted on 0171-512 7000.

Fidelity insurance

Fidelity insurance, also known as suretyship insurance, insures the honesty of trusted employees. The policy takes the forms of commercial guarantees or bonds. Such insurance is now rarely written, though still available.

Professional indemnity

Certain professional people such as accountants and lawyers must insure themselves against claims from clients.

Life, health and medical insurance

Your own life should be insured so that your family can survive after your death. The amount of cover depends on what dependants you have. A single person, or a widower with adult children, needs much less than a man with a young family. If you cannot afford normal whole life insurance, consider term insurance. This insures you against dying in, say, the next five years. If you survive those five years, nothing is paid. Term insurance is very cheap and is an effective way of giving needed cover.

It is not only death which can stop you working. A man in his forties can be up to 15 times as likely to suffer illness or disability that stops him working as he is to die. If this misfortune does hit you, there is the added expense of keeping you in addition to your family. Health insurance guarantees an income after a waiting period. The longer this period, the less your premium (or the greater your cover). The policy should be *permanent* health insurance (PHI). 'Permanent' means that you cannot be denied cover because of any change in your health after you take out the policy.

Medical insurance gives you private treatment, allowing you to avoid queues in the National Health Service or to convalesce in greater luxury. Despite horror stories in the press, the average wait for NHS treatment is less than five weeks. The insurance is now expensive for what you get. Unless you can arrange a large scheme for you and your employees, you can be better off not having it, and paying privately for treatment if necessary. Spend any money you save on PHI.

Keyman insurance

Keyman insurance allows a business to insure the life or health of any employee whose death or prolonged absence would cause the business to suffer. It is ordinary life or health insurance, but with the business as the beneficiary.

Note that you can insure the life of anyone on whom you depend. You only need to establish an 'insurable interest'. If you are in a partnership or a private company, there is usually a requirement for the remaining partners or members to buy out the interest of a partner or member who dies. This can also be covered by insurance.

Specific occupations

Certain businesses specifically require other types of insurance. For example, riding schools must insure liability for riders under the Riding Establishment Act 1970. Solicitors must have professional indemnity insurance under the Solicitors Act 1974. So must insurance brokers, under the Insurance Brokers (Registration) Act 1977. There are similar provisions for oil tankers, nuclear installations and keepers of wild animals.

Other Acts do not require insurance, but create a liability. For example, the Hotel Proprietors Act 1956 makes a hotelier liable for the loss of guests' property under certain circumstances. That risk can be insured.

16 Banking

Poor service

In 1991 banks were widely criticised for the poor service offered to small businesses. The criticisms were:

- charging interest rates which were too high and not passing on reductions in interest rates quickly and fully
- imposing extra charges without notice and
- general high-handedness.

They have subsequently been accused of imputing the wrong rate of interest. There are specific companies or computer programs which can check the amount charged by your bank.

The Office of Fair Trading found that the banks were not guilty of collusion. Codes of practice produced by the banks in 1991 and subsequently did little to assuage the anger of small businesses. Banks do offer a poor service to business. Newspapers routinely document cases of banks being arbitrary in calling in overdrafts, going back on their word, and imposing charges willy-nilly. Some banks will bounce a cheque for £30 and charge £25 for doing so.

Some businesses have found themselves like hostages to the bank, in a halfway house to liquidation where the bank's clearance must be sought for making expenditure. The banks can still tend to live in the old days when they regarded it as a privilege to allow you to bank with them, and where any loan was regarded as a favour to be received with gratitude. The idea that they are simply selling a service for a fee, like the shoe-mender, is not always evident in their approach.

A main problem is that local managers, who understand clients' needs best, are given insufficient discretion and authority to do their jobs properly. Instead, head offices are staffed by people inexperienced in dealing with customer relations. They make inflexible rules which simply alienate customers. If you are dissatisfied with the main banks, try Abbey National, Girobank, Cooperative Bank or a small bank.

Formalities

The mandate

To open a bank account for a business is similar to doing so as a private individual. For a limited company, the bank will want to see the certificate of incorporation and will require a formal board meeting minute.

There is a mandate which specifies who must sign and for what amount. Do not make it too complicated. At most have signatories up to a certain amount, and require no more than two signatories above. The mandate imposes little control on expenditure. Complex mandates and requirements for multiple signatures quickly become obstructive. Do not allow blank cheques. Nor have one signatory signing cheques awaiting a second signature. These defeat the whole purpose of the mandate controls. If you trust your accountant enough to let him hold blank cheques, make him a signatory.

Charges

Always clarify in advance what charges the bank intend to make and what interest they intend to charge. Do not be afraid to negotiate with the bank manager. In particular, discuss what rate will be charged for exceeding the overdraft. Insist on knowing all the annoying 'arrangement fees'. An arrangement fee is a charge for allowing the bank to sell you their service. Their existence is clear evidence of the 'we are doing you a favour' mentality, still prevalent in banks.

Periodically review the charges, comparing them with others

available. Look at other ways in which charges may be saved. There may be a cash management scheme in which funds on one account can reduce charges and interest on another, for example. Some accounting firms offer 'bank-busting' schemes which will do this for you.

Statements
Ensure that you have statements as frequently as needed, usually weekly or monthly. Also ensure that you have an adequate supply of cheque books.

Routine disciplines

Bank reconciliation
Periodically, usually every month, you should reconcile your bank statement to your cash book. The cash book will give you a figure of what you should have in the bank. This rarely agrees with the bank statement, because cheques and receipts have not yet been cleared. The steps in the bank reconciliation are broadly:

* identify items on the statement which do not appear in the cash book
* items such as bank charges and interest, and standing orders should be entered in the cash book
* identify items in the cash book which do not appear on the statement
* list these items. They should represent the difference between the cash figure and bank statement figure.

Also check that equivalent items are shown for the same amount. It is not unknown for a cheque to be cleared for a different amount from that in the cash book.

Discrepancies
The bank reconciliation is not just a bookkeeping exercise. It highlights irregularities that can require investigation. The most obvious example is a cheque that has 'bounced'. Charges and interest should

be compared with the figure that you expect, to ensure that they are not becoming excessive. Standing orders and direct debits can easily be overlooked. They should periodically be reviewed to see if the service they represent is really still needed.

Dishonoured cheques
If a cheque is dishonoured or 'bounced', you should immediately take appropriate action. If the cheque is dishonoured for some technical reason, give the customer the benefit of the doubt, the first time. Send the cheque back asking for a replacement, not a correction. Technical reasons are:

- words and figures disagree
- cheque not completed properly
- cheque not signed in accordance with mandate
- cheque is misdated.

Remember to adjust your cash book and sales ledger. If it happens again, be more cynical about whether the dishonour was unintended. It is known for companies deliberately to mis-sign cheques so that they are dishonoured, to give them a few extra days to pay.

If the cheque is marked 'return to drawer' or 'RD' or similar, it usually means that the customer has insufficient funds to clear the cheque. What you do depends on many factors, particularly what you know of the customer and what your relationship with him is (or was).

In other cases, you can protect your position by serving a default notice under Bills of Exchanges Act 1828. There is no particular form of words. Indeed, an oral notice is sufficient. The notice must identify the person who issued the cheque. The significance of this is that you can sue on a dishonoured cheque without having to prove liability. The only defence to dishonouring a cheque is duress (such as a gun to the head). The customer cannot argue that the goods were faulty or did not arrive or some such excuse.

17 Law

The following points detail some of the more important and relevant aspects of law as they affect small businesses. Readers should appreciate that the law can be very complex in all these areas. If a dispute arises, or you have to make a major decision based on a point of law, it is essential to obtain professional advice.

Freedom to contract

Every time you agree to supply goods or a service, and every time you agree to acquire goods or a service, you have made a contract. A contract does not have to be in writing. It is just as binding in law if made verbally or even implied from the conduct of the parties.

You do not have to make a contract with anyone. The fact that you offer goods or services for sale does not oblige you to sell them to any particular person. So you may simply refuse to supply a nuisance customer. Similarly a shopkeeper may bar a person he suspects of shoplifting, even though he cannot prove it. The exception to this freedom is that you may not discriminate on the grounds of sex or race.

The price

There is no general requirement to display prices on items for sale or on price lists, in catalogues or by another means. There are a few specific exceptions, such as most foodstuffs and drinks in pubs. However, if you do display the price, it must be the true price, including any VAT. There are specific regulations on how prices must be indicated on food and petrol.

If the price is conditional, the condition must be stated. The old practice of selling cars without saying that number plates are extra is outlawed. There are also restrictions on claiming that a price is discounted, reduced, below recommended price and the suchlike. You are not obliged to charge the same price for all payment methods. However, if you charge more for payment by credit cards, that fact must be clearly displayed.

If a mistake is accidentally made, you are not obliged to sell the goods at the incorrect price. So if the wrong price ticket is affixed to an item, or a number drops off the end of the price display on a car, you are safe. However, the error must be promptly corrected. If it keeps happening, you could have difficulties.

Suppliers may provide goods with prices on them. For medicines the supplier can enforce these prices. For other items, you do not have to follow the prices. Any attempt by a supplier to enforce a price is vigorously pursued by the Office of Fair Trading.

Quality of goods

If you sell goods, the Sale of Goods Act 1979 requires that:

- the goods are yours to sell
- any description is correct
- the goods are of 'merchantable quality' (of the quality a buyer would reasonably expect) and
- the goods are fit for the purpose for which they are sold.

If the goods do not meet these conditions, the customer can sue you for compensation. If the sale is to someone for their business purposes, you can contract out of any of these requirements. Otherwise, you may offer a guarantee giving a customer greater rights, but you cannot reduce his rights, even if the customer agrees.

If you misdescribe goods or services, you can be prosecuted under the Trade Descriptions Act 1968. There are also restrictions on wrongly describing goods in advertisements. These are enforced by the Advertising Standards Authority for printed advertisements, and by the relevant broadcasting authority for television and radio advertisements.

There is no general obligation to answer questions from customers or to make any representations about what you intend to supply. Neither are you obliged to let a potential customer inspect or test any item. It is legal to sell goods on a 'sold as seen' basis whereby the customer makes his own decision on what, if anything, he sees of the goods. However, if you *do* make any representation about the goods, you commit the offence of misrepresentation if that statement proves to be untrue.

Customer safety

The government has issued many regulations imposing specific safety requirements on certain goods. These particularly include clothes, items for children and items of intrinsic danger such as oil lamps. In addition, there is a general requirement for goods to be safe. However, the responsibility for unsafe goods generally rests with the manufacturer. If you sell a faulty ladder, you are liable to replace the ladder. The supplier is liable for any compensation to your injured customer.

Consumer credit

If you intend to let people pay for your goods or services by instalments on payment of interest, you must obtain a consumer credit licence from the Office of Fair Trading. All forms of hire purchase and leasing are included. There are different categories of licence depending on whether you are offering the credit yourself, or providing it in conjunction with a finance company. A licence lasts for five years.

You do not need a licence for imposing interest for late payment of an invoice, nor for allowing a discount for prompt payment or requiring a deposit before starting work. There is no obligation on any trader to offer trade terms to any customer. It is entirely a matter of commercial negotiation whether you allow customers to pay before or after you supply. In making your decision, you may use a credit reference agency to check on the customer. You do not need their permission to do this. However, if they ask you for the name of the agency used, you must provide it. You do not have to pass on details of what the agency said, and indeed will usually breach their conditions of supply if you do. Your customer has the right to write to the agency to see his file.

Theft

Theft is defined in the Theft Act 1968 s1 as 'dishonestly appropriate[ing] property belonging to another with the intention of permanently depriving the other of it'. So it is not theft if a person takes goods from a shop and leaves the money by a till. The shopkeeper can make him put the goods back as he has not agreed to sell them, but there is no theft as there is no dishonesty. Similarly, borrowing goods without permission is not theft, though the owner can again require their return.

A thief can be apprehended, by force if necessary. The practical problem is that you may be unsure whether the person has stolen. If you are wrong, you can be liable yourself for a whole range of offences including assault, unlawful imprisonment and slander. This is why store detectives often wait until the suspect has left the premises before apprehending him or her.

Data protection

If you keep information on computer about your customers, staff or anyone else, you must register with the Data Protection Registrar. A computerised mailing list or sales ledger does not in itself require registration, but other details, such as how well customers pay or disciplinary details of staff do require registration. Registration imposes a few restrictions which are unlikely to impede legitimate business.

Monopolies

Under fair trading legislation, a monopoly exists when a business controls 25 per cent of the supply or demand for a particular product or service. (A monopoly of demand is called a monopsony.) This brings the business within the ambit of the Monopolies and Mergers Commission (MMC) which ensures that the monopoly is not abusing its position by excluding competition, exploitative pricing or in a few other defined ways. The MMC can also in effect block mergers which create monopolies, or impose conditions on mergers.

The law allows competitors to co-operate in matters of mutual interest provided this does not work against the interest of customers. For example, you can join or form a trade association to promote your goods or services generally or to lobby the government on a pertinent issue. You generally may not form an agreement to carve up the market between you or to fix your prices collectively. Such an agreement is called a restrictive trade practice. Such a practice is not necessarily illegal. If there is a good reason for it, you can apply for it to be registered as such at the Office of Fair Trading.

Illegal selling methods

Generally, contract law assumes that buyer and seller stand eyeball to eyeball and are free to negotiate any contract they wish at whatever price they wish and on whatever terms they wish. If A secures a good deal at the expense of B, that is tough on B. The courts will enforce a properly made contract. They will not rectify a bad deal.

However, the reality is that buyer and seller frequently do not trade as equals. Often one has an unfair advantage over the other. The law therefore intervenes to restore some measure of equality in certain conditions.

Vulnerable buyers

A person under 18 may only contract for 'necessities' at a fair price and may not contract at all for any financial arrangement.

A person who suffers from a mental disorder may only contract to the extent that he is able to understand the contract at the time it was made, or agrees to ratify it during such a lucid interval. A contract cannot be made with someone whilst drunk. However, other emotions, such as tiredness or anger, do not invalidate a contract.

Any contract made under duress, that is by improper threats or blackmail, is void.

Doorstep selling

A sale in excess of £35 made off business premises, usually at a person's home, may be reversed by that person during a seven-day 'cooling-off' period. Most consumer credit agreements made off business premises are subject to a five-day cooling-off period.

Doorstep selling is not illegal, it is just subject to this additional safeguard.

Inertia selling

Inertia selling is when goods are sent to someone who has not ordered them and who is then pursued for payment. Under the Unsolicited Goods and Services Acts 1971 and 1975, the recipient must make reasonable efforts to protect the goods. He does not have to hire a warehouse, but neither can he deliberately leave the goods out in the rain. If no effort is made to reclaim the goods within six months, the recipient may have them as his own property. If the recipient writes to the supplier telling him he has received the goods, this period is reduced to 30 days. There must be an apparent intention that the recipient should keep them. It therefore does not allow someone to keep goods which have simply been sent to the wrong address by mistake.

For entries in directories, the position is even stricter. You only have to pay for an entry in a directory if you have signed a written order for it. You do not have to pay for entries made only by telephone, even if you have agreed to pay.

Any attempt to make someone pay for unsolicited goods or services is an offence.

Pyramid selling

Pyramid selling is when a distributor sells goods to other distributors to sell to others at progressively higher prices. The consequence is that the person at the bottom of the pyramid is obliged to buy goods which he cannot hope to sell because the price is high.

Pyramid selling is not illegal, but is strictly regulated. In particular:

- a new entrant may leave within seven days of joining
- an entrant may leave at any time requiring his distributor to buy back the goods for 90 per cent of the price paid for them
- it is an offence to state that a specific income can be earned
- there are limits on how much new recruits can pay for the goods.

Mail order

Advertisements selling goods must make it clear whether the sale is in the course of business. A furniture company cannot pretend to be an individual getting rid of his private furniture. A trade advertisement must clearly give the supplier's name and address.

There is no fixed time in which the goods must be supplied. The voluntary Advertising Standards Association code generally requires that they be supplied within four weeks.

Auctions

An auctioneer does not have to accept a bid. If he does, that is binding and neither party can back out. Goods may be auctioned with a reserve price, that is a price below which the auctioneer will not accept bids. Generally, all auction sales are 'sold as seen'. It is an offence under Mock Auctions Act 1961 to pretend that goods are being sold at a low price by deliberately selling a few items at a low price.

Shops

Shops must trade within set hours, as laid down in the Shops Acts. Generally:

- every shop must close by 8pm, except on Saturday or on another day chosen by the local authority when it must close at 9pm
- every shop must close at 1pm one weekday each week
- large shops can open for only six hours on Sundays but not on Easter Day.

There are exceptions to these rules, particularly for shops which sell food, medicines and motor accessories for immediate use. Regulations by local authorities may vary some hours such as early closing.

Terms and conditions

A contract has 'conditions' and 'warranties'. A condition is something which is essential to the agreement, such as the fact that the goods work. A warranty is something incidental to the agreement, such as when they will be supplied. Not meeting a condition allows the other party to regard the contract as ended and claim damages. Not meeting a warranty only allows a claim for damages.

It is common practice for each party to try to impose its own conditions (beneficial to its own position) on the other party. This is done by printing them on the back of forms and stating that those conditions take precedence over all others. Generally, the courts seem to hold the set which was last 'imposed' on the other side as final. The reality is that businessmen seem unconcerned with law as any dispute is negotiated anyway.

The Unfair Contract Terms Act 1977 limits the extent to which a business may rely on printed conditions. It makes it impossible to contract out of any liability for death or personal injury. Other clauses which seek to avoid liability are only effective to the extent that they are reasonable.

Copyright and patents

As well as acquiring physical property such as buildings and

154

premises, you may acquire 'intellectual property' such as copyrights and patents. These also need to be protected.

A patent is taken out for a new invention which is original and not obvious. It is a form of contract between you and the state. For sharing your idea with the world, you are allowed exclusive use of it for 20 years.

Copyright is not registered. As soon as you create a library, artistic or musical work, it is copyright to you. Sometimes authors, artists and composers have their work notarised by a solicitor, so that they can later prove that they had created the work when they said they had. The work need not have any aesthetic value. A directory or instruction manual is copyright as a work of literature. There is no copyright in ideas or information, but there is in words. Copyright can be avoided simply by rephrasing text.

Copyright lasts for its creator's lifetime and 75 (previously 50) years thereafter.

Defamation

Defamation is publishing a statement which reduces a reputation below that which a reasonable person should hold. Generally, publishing a true statement cannot be defamatory as it just reduces a reputation to what it should be. Defamation is libel if in permanent recorded form, such as writing or film. It is slander if spoken. Slander is much rarer, because the defamed person must prove financial loss.

Defamation does not have to be malicious. An honest work or even a work of fiction can be libellous. Libel can also be by insinuation. It is not the literal meaning of words which matter, but what an ordinary man will understand. It is also possible to sue for malicious falsehood. This is an untrue statement which causes loss, but is not defamatory. A common example is saying that someone has ceased trading.

In English law, only a living person or his trade may be libelled. Under Scots law, libel and slander are one offence. Defamation covers injury to feelings and statements made to the person about himself. There is also a ragbag of similar old offences still illegal though rarely prosecuted, such as criminal libel (threatening a breach of peace), scandalising a court, blasphemy, sedition, and obscene libel.

Wrongful and fraudulent trading

It is an offence for a company to trade when you know, or should know, that your creditors are unlikely to be paid. It is not an offence to be naively optimistic or unreasonably to believe that the sunshine of good fortune may yet dawn on your enterprise.

Fraudulent trading is when it can be proved beyond reasonable doubt that the business was run to defraud, such as by taking payments for goods you cannot supply. All directors and anyone else involved are liable for criminal penalties and to pay restitution.

Wrongful trading is when the directors have been irresponsible in how they run the business which becomes insolvent. An example is paying themselves excessive fees in preference to paying the bills. It also makes the directors personally liable for the debts.

Fraudulent trading and wrongful trading will usually bar a person from holding any directorship for many years.

18 Human skills

The importance

Most people would admit to not having enough time to do the things they want to do. Going self-employed will increase pressure on your time and will cause conflict of interest regarding priorities.

Those contemplating self-employment who make time to think about time often reach startling, far-reaching conclusions. After going self-employed you may not be able to spend enough of your time doing the things that you consider important, such as time with your family or pursuing hobbies like music or sport. Although you are working at a frantic pace, you are not really achieving anything: deadlines get missed and competitors are getting more business than you.

Three vital areas

Those who have succeeded in organising their time and their life to better effect have concentrated on three areas that are vital for both those contemplating self-employment and those already self-employed.

First, you must identify what you want out of life and self-employment and translate this into life goals, career goals and short-term goals. This will clarify what is important to you. It will give you a framework against which you can put a priority on your use of time.

Second, you must turn your attention to achieving more of your priorities through more effective time and self management. Once you have established priorities in your work and leisure, it is possible to review how well you have organised yourself in the past to meet them. There is nothing to suggest that if you have been disorganised in the past you will become organised becoming self-employed.

You will need to carry out an in-depth and honest analysis of your past time planning to determine your personal strengths and weaknesses. Having carried this out you will have created a personal 'time profile' that will highlight areas for improvement in your planning. Then, when planning, you will be able to ensure that you allocate time to priority activities. For instance if you consider it a priority to spend more time creating a business plan for the bank manager you can build such time into your future plans, not merely hope that the opportunity will turn up. In the same way, if your family is a priority you can build family time into your schedules.

Third, if you are to make most use of your time you will need to concentrate on your levels of physical and mental fitness and physical and mental stamina. If your body cannot stay the course, self-employment will become a trial. You cannot afford to put in anything less than 110 per cent effort and you cannot afford to become ill. In much the same way, your mind must demonstrate reserves of fitness and stamina to enable you to analyse and solve the many business problems that will undoubtedly occur. Your decisions and future success will very much depend on sustained levels of innovative, analytical and creative thought.

Life planning

Time is our most valuable asset, yet we tend to think more about how we spend our money than how we spend our time. Money can be stored and invested for future use and if it becomes scarce it is possible to earn, beg, steal or borrow more. None of these things can be done with time.

You must be clear on your life priorities and goals prior to becoming self-employed and you must be committed to reviewing them on a regular basis thereafter. To test your current level of thinking get a piece of paper now and answer the following questions:

1   What are the six most important areas of your life? (These may include such things as health, wealth, family, business, football etc.)
2   If you were told today that you only had six months to live, what would be your priorities for that remaining time?
3   If in answer to a wish, you were told that your one overriding ambition could be achieved without any fear of failure or lack of resources, what would that ambition be?

In answering these questions you have gone some way towards identifying your life goals and priorities. Let us look at each question in turn and analyse your answers.

Question 1. If you had trouble in immediately identifying the six most important areas of your life, it is an indication that you have not previously given it enough thought. In which case, how are you currently identifying the priorities in your life? Are you merely reacting, taking things as they come, or regretting things not done because there was not enough time. You must determine prior to self-employment, and review on a regular basis thereafter, the six or more priorities in your life. Review the list now, discuss it with your family and decide on the order of precedence.

Life is about maintaining a fine balance between all the areas on your list. If in the future you spend long hours working (which will become a certainty when you become self-employed), you must redress the balance by, for example, building time into your future schedule for your family. In this way you will maintain your life priorities and gain the satisfaction that you are spending your time wisely. Too many people have regrets over time ill spent. You cannot go back and try again; you have only one chance to get it right. Prioritise your life goals now and review them on a regular basis.

Question 2. In answer to this question you may have identified such things as world travel, financial security for your family, visiting friends and relations, retirement to the country etc. Whatever your answers, they are a further indication of your personal and family priorities. What have you done in the past to satisfy these priorities? Are they just things that are in the future? In which case, they may remain so! Is this what you want? Self-employment will become a large priority in your time planning and there is a danger that the things you have listed will become forgotten and of low priority.

The truth is that you never know when you only have six months to live. Self-employment or any other factor should not cause you to ignore or forget your priorities. Determine immediately to provide for your family's future, write a Will, make up a 'death and disaster' folder providing information on bank accounts, insurance policies, pensions, how to change a plug and where to find the stopcock in an emergency. Build time into your future plans for some element of travel and find time to visit friends and relations.

Question 3. If you have a long held ambition it is likely, in the circumstances, to be a wish to run your own company. Alternatively, you may have a desire to play a musical instrument or win a major sporting event. Whatever your long held ambition, there is no doubt that, given the powers we possess of mind over matter, your ambition could be fulfilled. At what cost, however?

Almost certainly the cost will be the balance you are maintaining between your priorities. Is this a cost you and your family are prepared to pay? Outstanding success as a self-employed businessman or woman can be achieved by dedicating large amounts of your time to it at the expense of other priorities. On the other hand, measured success can be balanced against your other priorities and can lead to a great deal of satisfaction from achievements made with the support of family and loved ones. Self-employment is hard enough without alienating those around you.

Set your priorities and life goals now!

Strengths and weaknesses

There is no reason to assume that poor planning in your current employment will automatically be transformed when you become self-employed. The pressures on you will be increased. The levels of self-discipline needed to plan your time effectively will be significantly greater.

Remember, particularly when you start, there will be no one

behind you to get you going in the morning, no one to pester you for your plans, no one to insist you prioritise and no one to ensure you meet deadlines. You must be self-motivated and must ensure that you have the self-discipline needed to be efficient in your use of time and effective and professional in the provision of your goods or services.

Questions
Answer the following questions as the first step in determining your personal strengths and weaknesses.

1 How much of what you do at work is planned, and how much just happens?
2 When do you plan your day? Your week? Your month?
3 Do you allocate priorities to your planned tasks, or tackle them as they occur?
4 How effective is your planning?
5 Are you easily distracted by bits of paper, trivial thoughts, other priorities or the postman coming to the door?
6 How strong are your powers of concentration?
7 Do you get satisfaction from managing sudden unexpected crises?
8 Are you satisfied that you achieve something important and productive most days?
9 Are you able to finish tasks within the time you allocated?
10 Do you get the vital jobs right or do you try to get everything correct?
11 Do you find a reason to talk to someone, get another cup of coffee or read the newspaper again when you're bored?
12 Are you decisive?
13 What tasks do you put off or avoid altogether?
14 Are you an effective communicator? Are you concise and direct or ambiguous?
15 How assertive are you in dealing with clients and officialdom? Can you say '*No*' when you have conflicting priorities?
16 Can you cope with long working hours and do you amend priorities accordingly?
17 Are you clear on the 'make or break' areas of your work and have you identified the priority tasks?

18 Are you able to get information you need to carry out your job well, and are you analytical and decisive?
19 At what times of the day are you most alert and active mentally and physically?
20 If you could create free time at work, how would you use it?

Now you have answered these questions yourself you need to check your objectivity, particularly where your own skills or lack of them is concerned. Ask someone who knows how you work to answer as many of the questions as they can, giving their honest opinion of your natural behaviour and work style. Analysis will now indicate your strengths and weaknesses and you will be able to plan your ongoing self-development for successful self-employment.

In your analysis consider the following important principles regarding each question:

Questions 1 and 2 refer to planning and whether you regularly make time to plan your work and leisure. It must be a daily habit to plan not only the day but your week, month and year, if necessary. Not only must you plan but you must prioritise in accordance with your analysis of goals and Key Result Areas.

Questions 3 and 4 need you to assess your current habits and really question your current effectiveness. Are you satisfied? If there is any doubt, undertake self-improvement or question your suitability for self-employment.

Questions 5 and 6 measure your powers of concentration which must be high to cover the amount of work you will almost certainly be expected to complete on self-employment. If you are easily distracted, decide where you can work without distraction and learn to increase your powers of concentration. Your front room table may not be the ideal location, particularly when the children are on half-term leave.

Some people enjoy handling crises, perhaps at the expense of other priorities. The fact that it is a crisis may not make it a priority. Analyse and then determine its relative importance. If your answer to *Question 7* is positive you may need to question your strength of mind in sticking to the important jobs. A positive answer to *Question 8* would suggest that you employ a disciplined routine to carrying out your work. Keep it up!

Question 9 refers to your estimation of times when allocating your effort. It may be that as a perfectionist you are spending too much time with the detail (*Question 10*). Allocate effort in accordance with priority and ensure you stick to your plans.

Do you get bored easily or stick at it? Be honest with *Question 11* and make an assessment of your power to apply yourself. Short breaks may well be therapeutic but engaging others in discussing the pleasures of golf may well lead to missed deadlines.

Time spent agonising over decisions (*Question 12*) may well lead to other work taking a back seat. Can you afford the time? If so fine, if not, make your decision, be committed and move on!

If your prioritisation is based on relative enjoyment you will find a long list as a result of *Question 13*. Only put off non-urgent tasks (but plan them) and tasks that are trivial in relation to the work. Otherwise put personal preference aside, get on with the important tasks even though they may be unpleasant. You will get a heightened sense of achievement when they are finished.

The successful self-employed are effective communicators, concise and direct. Consider other people's answers to *Question 14*, it may be difficult for you to be objective. If they consider you to be verbose, learn to become a more effective communicator. You may not have the time for long chats at each customer's office.

Your assertiveness is examined in *Question 15*. Can you leave when you choose without causing offence? Can you end rambling conversations without appearing rude? Can you say '*No*' when you have other jobs to get on with? You cannot offend customers but it is imperative that you get on with your work.

Your 'Life Planning' is reaffirmed in *Question 16*. Get it right, it's too important not to.

Question 17 refers once again to your priorities, particularly associated with work. If you are not sure, take time to carry out the analysis detailed in the next chapter to determine make-or-break areas, otherwise referred to as 'Key Result Areas'.

Check your capability to be analytical and decisive in answer to *Question 18*. Do you consider information-gathering a priority? You should do. Too many self-employed are so busy getting on with the work that they miss new opportunities in technology, are unaware of new markets and ignore the aggressive market newcomer. Keep up to date, gather information and analyse the implications for your business. Carry this out on a regular basis and make time for it in your plans.

Question 19 refers to what are sometimes called biorhythms. Basically, are you a morning or afternoon person, when do you feel more mentally alert and when are your powers of concentration best? These are the times you should plan to work on your priorities.

Finally, with the time you have created, plan to carry out the tasks identified in *Question 20*. You cannot afford to sit around basking in the glory of your improved planning. Not yet, anyway!

Now, re-confirm those weaknesses and do something about them. In self-employment, there is no place for complacency. Strive constantly to improve both yourself and the company's performance.

Congratulations on completing your personal 'Time Profile'.

Physical and mental fitness and stamina

Physical fitness

If you are too tired after a day's work to sit down and work out your VAT return, or would prefer to sit in a chair rather than visit that potential customer, you may be suffering fatigue. While an employer may tolerate occasional days off, they will cause your own business to suffer.

These examples are a function of physical fitness and stamina – yours! Are you as fit as you should be in order to undertake the rigours of self-employment? You cannot choose to ignore requests to review potential work, even though those requests may come outside normal working hours, and you certainly cannot afford to lose time through avoidable illness.

Determine now to improve your levels of physical fitness and stamina. You will notice an improvement in your life. Your zest for business will make you unbeatable. Undertake regular exercise. Lose weight if you need to, and you will suffer less from minor ailments. Include regular exercise in your daily plans. Done regularly, exercise can become a pleasure.

If your chosen job is office or home based requiring substantial time to be spent at a typewriter or computer, make a point of going out into the fresh air at least once a day. Physical fitness and stamina will give you the energy to fulfil all your personal and business goals whilst maintaining a fast pace. All successful self-employed people find time to keep their bodies at peak levels of efficiency. They are, after all the main tools of your trade.

Mental fitness

Of equal importance to physical fitness is the mental fitness and stamina we possess. Levels of concentration, the ability to solve problems, analyse marketing strategies and determine the strength of the opposition all depend on the capacity of our minds to undertake complex thought. This may not only apply when we consider ourselves at our best, perhaps in the mornings, but on returning home after a hard day at work when a quotation needs to be provided urgently for our best customer.

If your brain currently starts to hurt after 15 minutes of concentrated work, it may be a sign that you should improve on your levels of mental fitness and stamina. Your last employment may not have required a great deal of innovative or analytical thought: after all, you had done it for a number of years and had gained the experience to react to most problems without too much thought. As a result, your brain, whilst possessing lightning reactions, lost the capacity for substantial bursts of creative thinking.

The brain is similar to other muscles in your body in that if used infrequently it will gradually become flabby. If you have been unlucky enough to have a limb in plaster for any length of time you will appreciate that muscles must be strengthened when the plaster is removed. In the same way, the brain must be exposed in order to exercise to strengthen its capacity and efficiency.

Brainstorming

The finest exercise for improving brain fitness and consequently stamina has been found to be brainstorming. This exercise is more often than not associated with a group session, where team members feed off the ideas of their colleagues. The brainstorming referred to here is, however, a solo activity and requires more energy as a result.

Prior to discussing the technique it is necessary to understand some of the workings of the brain, particularly the section known as the memory. Firstly, the memory is not like an audio or video tape where data is stored in sequence. If this were the case, it would be easy to refer to past events and areas of learning by means of a reference number or perhaps something like a library code. In fact the memory only links data by a loose system of association that is sometimes referred to as a mind map. Association is the reason that certain tunes will remind us of pleasurable events when perhaps the tune was playing in the background, or why we remember names when the person is in the environment where we expect to see them. Meet someone in a strange place and whilst we know the face, the name escapes us.

Brainstorming makes use of association and imposes a discipline on us to visualise everything we currently have stored in the memory. The exercise is therefore a valid one in that we can use it on any occasion when we need to recall facts and figures from memory. For instance, when preparing a report it would be useful to put all known facts on paper and then sort them into chapters. We will also explore in the next chapter how brainstorming can greatly assist the planning process.

So when you are brainstorming get a large piece of paper and first set the objective for the exercise. As an example, brainstorm all the equipment, food, clothing and accessories you would need for a weekend holiday in the New Forest or Yorkshire Dales. With this as the objective, commence and continue to write down whatever comes into your head. Write down everything, even though you may not consider it to be relevant. This is important because this is association at work. If you fail to write everything down, you will break the chain of association and information, perhaps vital, further along the chain may not emerge and as a result be forgotten. When you finish, you may well be mentally tired, but you will be impressed at the quality and quantity of data available to you. You can now sort it out and successfully plan your weekend away in the knowledge that you haven't forgotten anything vital.

Not only is brainstorming a fine mental exercise, it also has many practical applications, particularly for the self-employed. For instance, brainstorming a marketing plan, ensuring everything has been included in a business plan, preparing a list of work for a particular project or determining all the important factors prior to deciding to going self-employed.

19 Management

Introduction

Management at its simplest level is the skills needed to run a business. It involves:

- vision
- reality
- decision-making
- delegation
- communication
- negotiation and
- control.

Vision

You start with a dream. You start with images of wealth, power, success, recognition, usefulness – or whatever else matters to you. You may not always reach your destination, but knowing where it is considerably improves your chances. This is not some pie-in-the-sky modern idealism. It is simply extending the accounting principle of budgeting into the non-financial areas of business.

Reality

Reality is the counterbalance to vision. It is easy to become so obsessed with a vision of the promised land that you forget to bring the bus fare. You need the 'street knowledge' of your business. If your head is in the clouds, at least keep your feet on the ground. Never turn your back on any aspect of your business.

Decision-making

Introduction
The ability to make a decision lies at the heart of management. If you are the sort of person who, when asked 'Would you like a cup of coffee?' replies 'Well, are you having one?' or 'Well, if its' not too much trouble', or similar, you are not a manager. Whether the other person is having coffee is irrelevant. Asking if it's too much trouble is fatuous, as the person has already offered.

There are six steps to making any decision:

- clarify your objective
- consider the factors which influence your choice
- compile a list of options
- consider the consequences of the options
- compare the options and make the choice
- do it.

Clarify the objective
Clarify the objective into the simplest form. The decision is not how to get gas cylinders to the top floor. The decision may be how to get fuel for bunsen burners to your laboratory. This more basic decision opens up more options: putting the laboratory on the ground floor, piping up the gas, replacing the bunsen burners.

You never have an objective of employing someone. You may have an objective of how to get something done. Employing someone is one solution.

Consider the factors which influence your choice
First, identify any constraints. If you want to do some new process in-house, will you need a licence? Will you get planning permission? Do you have enough space? There is no point in considering options which cannot be implemented.

Finance is usually a factor. All financial elements can be reduced to a single consideration. For example, suppose option A involves spending £20,000 now, while option B involves spending £3,000 a year indefinitely. How much would £20,000 on deposit allow you to spend each year? If the answer is £2,000, option B becomes directly comparable to option A, and is seen to be more expensive.

If there is some doubt about the outcome of an option, it may be appropriate to use probability factors. These are numbers between 0 and 1 which represent how likely something is. For example if there is a 40 per cent chance an option will cost £10,000, and a 60 per cent chance it will cost £20,000, the 'probable' cost is:

$$0.4 \times £10,000 = £4,000$$
$$0.6 \times £20,000 = \underline{£12,000}$$
$$£16,000$$

Having identified all the factors, list them as advantages or disadvantages. If, exceptionally, you find that all factors emerge as advantages or disadvantages, you have no decision to make. You have a foregone conclusion.

Many factors will be both advantages and disadvantages. New equipment may save you time, but make your workspace more cluttered. When this happens, consider each factor separately, and decide overall whether it is an advantage or disadvantage.

Compile a list of options
From the list of advantages and disadvantages, prepare a list of possible options to meet your basic objective. Usually you will want to include the 'do nothing' option. The implication of not meeting your objective at all helps evaluate other options.

The process of brainstorming can be very effective here. A group of people can bounce ideas off each other. Many silly and frivolous ideas will come out, but that does not matter. Brainstorming is a process whereby the collective intelligence is greater than the sum of the parts. One person may suggest a frivolous solution which includes a novel approach to a problem. That novel approach can be adopted without the frivolity. Adopting a dog does not oblige you to adopt all its fleas.

The compilation stage should quickly eliminate many options. It is unlikely that you will need to go forward with more than three options.

Consider the consequences of the options
Having come up with a shortlist of options, consider the consequences of the option. How will the workforce react? How will this affect the company's image? Is the computer system adequate?

It is a common mistake to confuse factors with consequences. A factor is something which is so fundamental to the option that it influences *whether* to proceed. A consequence is not fundamental and does not influence whether to proceed, but does influence *how* to proceed. If you confuse factors and consequences you will never decide anything.

The opposite problem is to ignore consequences. That is a recipe for disaster. All change is disruptive. That does not make it wrong, but it does mean it needs considering.

Compare the options and make the choice
Various methods have been developed for making the choice. One method is to allocate points to each option according to each factor, perhaps by using the numbers 1 to 5, with a lower top score for the less important factors. The danger with this is that it introduces a spurious accuracy. Another method is the decision matrix. The options are listed horizontally and the objectives vertically. You then tick the boxes as each option meets the objectives. Sometimes the lists of advantages and disadvantages is good enough.

Occasionally, two options will emerge as equal winners. The procedure here is to look at the less important factors to make the decision. Perhaps one machine is a little less noisy. Perhaps sub-contracting rather than doing a job in-house will put you in a better position for negotiating a price for further sub-contract work. By treating the most important consequence as a factor, the decision can be made.

Sometimes there is just no winner. What time should you meet? What should a new product be called? There may be no obvious answer and no way of finding it. If the decision is arbitrary, be arbitrary.

Choose anything. Remember that the cost of indecision often exceeds the cost of decision. For example, an item needs repainting to prevent rot. What colour should it be painted? Painting it red, then deciding it should be green, may be cheaper than letting it rot while you reach the decision that it should be green. Many decisions involving maintenance and dispute-resolution will come into this category. Be arbitrary with conviction.

These processes can usually be completed in a few minutes if you do them yourself. If you involve others, make it clear that they are there in an advisory capacity and not an executive one. The decision must still be yours alone, unless the business structure requires that decision to be collective.

Do it
The final part of any decision-making is to implement the decision. Some management books include communicating the decision as an additional step. It may sound silly including 'do it' as part of the process. (Even doing nothing is 'doing it' if that is your decision.) But in reality many decisions are never implemented.

Some short cuts

Some business decisions are made so routinely that the decision-making process can be short-circuited.

Stock holding
Under the Pareto principle, 20 per cent of your stock comprises about 80 per cent of the value. This principle has proved remarkably constant in widely varying circumstances. Control that 20 per cent only. For the other 80 per cent, keep a good quantity always in stock.

Keep a good supply of stationery and all other routine consumables. By withholding spending of stationery of £100, you may save £10 a year. When you find that you cannot photocopy urgently needed documents because you have no toner, the cost is much greater.

Tooling
If a piece of equipment or software which would be used every day

is needed, buy it. Time saved in this way almost always cost-justifies itself.

Company cars
If you have company cars, there is a formula for working out when to replace them. The answer is always the same: every two years. If you have a fleet of vehicles, you have the choice of using a fleet vehicle management company or doing it yourself. There is no difference in total cost. Decide according to whether you want to handle the matter yourself.

Delegation

Delegation is the next most important management ability after decision-making. When you start a business, you do much or even everything yourself. As your business expands, you must let go and pass work to other people. These will be either sub-contractors (people in business to provide that service) or employees. That is a decision which you must make. How to deal with employees is discussed in the next chapter. Delegate a clearly defined area of responsibility. Never delegate all financial control. You must always remain in charge of the cheque book. Many small businesses have been ruined by fraud.

You get part of the system exactly as you want it, and pass it over to someone. You start with the most mundane and routine duties. Not only are these the easiest to delegate, they are also the cheapest to employ people for. Many small businesses find handing over even mundane jobs very difficult. You must let go. Keep an eye on your new employee or sub-contractor, but let him get on with the job. Allow for the fact that another person may work efficiently by making minor changes in how the job is done.

As a manager, you should present yourself as a team-leader rather than a dictator. Let them share the ups and downs of your business. Make them feel they belong. Delegate one function at a time.

Communication

Communication is an important business skill, yet many managers have done nothing to improve their speaking, reading and writing ability since early schooldays. Communication is vital to how you present your company, how successful you are with regulatory authorities, how successful you are at negotiations, and how you keep your staff together.

The impact of spoken communication has been reckoned as:

* 55 per cent body language
* 48 per cent how you say it and
* only 7 per cent what you are saying.

The study of body language and communication skills will reward most managers. The rudiments are to be:

* clear
* concise
* correct and informed
* positive
* friendly.

Negotiation

Negotiation is a form of communication. You are attempting to resolve or agree something with someone who does not agree with you.

The first step is to find the common ground. Often you both want to achieve something, but differ on the methods. There is only one prerequisite to achieving an agreement: you both want to do so. Having identified the common ground, identify the areas of disagreement. There are only three ways of resolving any dispute:

* concession
* conciliation and
* confrontation.

You consider them in this order. Concession is where you give in because you consider the dispute is of insufficient importance. Conciliation is where you trade one disadvantage for another. Confrontation is where you fight. Negotiation should be kept in conciliation. Give nothing away as concession. Keep it as a bargaining counter. Avoid confrontation. Only launch into battle if you have the stamina, time, determination and resources to fight to win. The fact that you are right is not a good enough reason to fight. After the Battle of Waterloo, the Duke of Wellington said, 'The next worst thing to losing a battle is to win it.' Businessmen don't need pyrrhic victories and battle scars.

The only two methods of negotiating are:

- horse-trading and
- chip bargaining.

Horse-trading is where you narrow the difference by moving a little towards each other. Chip bargaining is where you give in on one point if the other party gives in on another. Here you must look for areas which matter little to you, but much to the other party. With communication skills you make a little concession seem like a big one in order to get a big concession back. Apologising and offering amends for some trivial indiscretion is often a good tactic.

There are certain methods for speeding up the deadline or breaking a deadlock as follows.

The *deadline* concentrates the mind by imposing a time limit on your discussions.

Feigned disinterest is where you prompt the other person to move by pretending that you don't really care if it all falls through.

The *what if?* strategy breaks a deadlock. You can suggest, 'What if we double the order?' 'What if we pay in advance?' 'What if we see how things work out over the next three months?'

Hawk and dove is when two of you negotiate. The hawk is the hard man who browbeats the other side. Then he leaves the room, and the dove offers a quick deal. The method was originally developed for torturing prisoners, but don't let that discourage you. It is an old trick, but it still works.

A *recess* allows the two sides to reflect on their position. It allows each side to reconsider its position and to be a little more yielding without losing face. Remember the Kennedy strategy (after the American President). To win an argument, you must allow the other side a face-saving way out.

Delegation breaks a deadlock by passing a 'detail' to junior colleagues. The detail may actually be the essence of the negotiation.

The *golf club* strategy is where the matter is passed up, or dealt with in a less formal atmosphere.

Each of these strategies works in appropriate circumstances. Each can make matters worse in the wrong circumstances. Whatever you have agreed, put it in writing promptly and make sure it is agreed by all parties. The most honest man can start believing you agreed what he wanted you to agree.

Control

Keep control on all the key aspects of your business. The rudiments of management control are:

- stating the principles of the business
- communicating those principles
- promoting those principles
- monitoring compliance with those principles
- monitoring the principles themselves and
- dealing with non-compliance.

A particular area of control is the resources available to the business. There are three:

- money
- expertise and
- the idea.

And that is the order of priority for controlling them.

Classical management principles

There are many books readily available on management, as well as biographies by successful managers. Most of them are worth a read. They can be quite entertaining and make a pleasant way of passing a train or aeroplane journey. A few of the recognised management principles are included below.

Classical principles of management

In 1916 Henri Fayol said that management should be based on 14 principles. These were codified by Lyndall Urwick as:

1   division of work and responsibility
2   authority matching responsibility
3   discipline
4   unity of command (each worker has one boss)
5   unity of direction
6   subordination of interest to the general interest
7   remuneration which is fair reward for effort
8   centralisation
9   scalar or hierarchical principle of line authority (i.e. line management)
10 principle of order (a place for everyone and everything in its place)
11 equity
12 stability of tenure of personnel
13 importance of initiative and
14 importance of esprit de corps.

Today, number 6 is more likely to be replaced by motivation.

The Winning Streak

The book *The Winning Streak* by Walter Goldsmith and David Clutterbuck (Weidenfeld and Nicolson) identified eight areas essential to business success:

1   leadership (clearly visible individuals, clear policy)

2   autonomy (little centralisation, decisions passed down the line)
3   control (very tight control in areas that matter, freedom in other areas)
4   involvement (the staff are made to feel it is 'their' company)
5   market orientation (the 'customer is king' philosophy)
6   zero-basing (keeping to what you know how to do. The opposite is known as 'buy a cow' from the expression 'If you want a glass of milk, buy a cow')
7   innovation (constant interest in how all aspects may be changed) and
8   integrity (fair dealing ultimately pays off).

Twenty commandments
R W Holder in his entertaining book *Thinking About Management* (Bath University Press) gives 20 commandments. Although a little tongue-in-cheek and aimed more at larger companies, his advice is still relevant to small businesses:

1   Never sell a new product to a new customer.
2   Always look for a customer who isn't spending his own money.
3   Never ask for any figures which are not also necessary for running the business.
4   Never let an accountant circulate any accounts which the rest of the management cannot understand.
5   Never trust computer-based spreadsheets.
6   Never try to bilk an agent of his commission.
7   Do not give open credit to foreigners.
8   Never place an outside order for anything yourself.
9   Do not tie up your working capital in fixed assets, which are later restated. Never use an overdraft for hard-core borrowing.
10   Never commit any resources to plant and machinery without understanding why.
11   Never expect your juniors to be as smart and dedicated as you are yourself.
12   Never start a development programme which cannot be funded from current production.
13   Never choose a new location on the basis of incentives.

14 Never pledge the credit of your parent company for an operation abroad.
15 Never overlook anyone who performs well in a junior function.
16 Aim your publicity at customers.
17 Never engage in contentious litigation.
18 Never exceed your overdraft limit without first warning your bank.
19 Never go back once you've left.
20 If you stop enjoying your job, leave it.

'Laws'

In 1955 C Northcote Parkinson published his famous *Parkinson's Law*. This was based on serious research and is well-documented in his books. They are also very entertaining. His style has been much copied. Some of the more apposite 'laws' are given below:

- Parkinson's Law: work expands to fill the time available for its completeness.
- Parkinson's Second Law: expenditure rises to fill income.
- Parkinson's Third Law: growth leads to complexity, complexity to decay.
- Parkinson's Fourth Law: delay is the deadliest form of denial.
- Murphy's Law: if anything can go wrong, it will.
- Metz's Law: Being the boss doesn't make you right. It only makes you the boss.
- Peter Principle: In a hierarchy, every employee tends to rise to his level of incompetency.

20 Staff

Recruitment

You are generally free to recruit staff as you wish. You can use the JobCentre, a card in a local newsagent, an advertisement in a newspaper or an employment agency. An agency is only likely to be needed where you have need for a particular skill.

Do not overlook the opportunities for having someone working for a few hours a week. Part-time work is now becoming very popular. There are many skilled people who cannot work full hours. Also, do not overlook the opportunity of engaging someone running their own business.

You are not allowed to discriminate on the grounds of sex or race (with a few exceptions). You must not discriminate on the grounds that a person is or is not a member of a trade union. In Northern Ireland you are not allowed to discriminate on grounds of religion. Otherwise you may make your choice on any other basis.

It is tempting when you first need to engage someone, to help out any friends or relations who are unemployed. Be careful. You must always be in a position where you can discipline or even dismiss your staff, if necessary. Think through the consequences of disciplining or dismissing your father-in-law before giving him work. There is also a risk that a friend will see his work as an opportunity for socialising with you.

Calculating

Whoever you engage or employ will not be as committed to the work as you are. Their loyalty is to their next pay cheque, not to you. But this need not be a problem.

Remember that engaging someone for 37 hours a week does not mean that you will get 37 x 52 = 1,924 hours work out of them every year. They will probably have four weeks' holiday plus public holidays. At any time, 5 per cent of your workforce will (on average) be away sick. In any year, 4 per cent of your female staff will be pregnant (requiring at least 18 weeks' absence). They will also be late, have periods with no work to do, and so on. A full-time worker provides about 1,000 hours of actual work a year. If you use that figure, you will not go far wrong.

Also, remember that an employee costs you more than his or her salary. There is national insurance of 10 per cent on top (12.2 per cent from 1999/00), plus extra overheads of floor space, refreshments and suchlike. The overheads are rarely less than 50 per cent of salary. For a sales rep with a company car and needing office support, it can be 200 per cent of salary. So if you engage a full-time worker for £10,000 a year, he or she is costing you about £15 an hour, even though the official hourly rate is about £5 an hour.

Legal requirements

There are many legal requirements regarding employment. The following is a summary of the main ones.

If a person is employed by you, as opposed to being self-employed and engaged by you, you must register for PAYE. This includes casual staff.

You are 'vicariously liable' for the acts of your employees while working for you.

You must insure them against injury, death or illness incurred in their work.

There are specific laws about working conditions and safety. You must provide each employee with a chair; there must be drinking water and toilet facilities; equipment must be safe; and the temperature must be at least 61°F. There are many other conditions.

An employee must be given a written contract of employment

within two months, outlining the basic conditions of work.

If an employee is sick or pregnant you must pay statutory sick pay or statutory maternity pay under the rules of the scheme. Remember that you may be able to claim some of this back under the PAYE system. Otherwise the only liability you have to pay an employee for sickness, maternity or holidays is what you agree in the contract.

You may instruct an employee to do work only within the ambit of what he was engaged to do. A clerk cannot be ordered to deliver goods. You can ask him and he may agree, but you cannot order him.

The employee must be paid his wages on time by the agreed method and given a payslip. You can only deduct items from wages if:

- authorised by statute (e.g. tax and national insurance)
- authorised by the employee (e.g. trade union dues or pension fund contributions)
- to correct a mistake in a previous payslip (though not all such mistakes are reclaimable)
- required by a court under an attachment of earnings order or similar or
- to compensate for a loss of stock or takings in a retail trade. You may deduct the loss up to 10 per cent of the employee's wages. You have to prove that the takings or stock was lost during the employee's shift. You do not have to prove that the employee took it.

You must give employees time off for ante-natal care, to look for alternative work if made redundant, and for jury service and to discharge certain other public duties (such as being a magistrate).

Employees are free to join or not join a trade union as they wish. However, you do not have to recognise or negotiate with any trade union unless you wish to do so.

Motivation

Staff must be motivated to work most efficiently. Motivators are classified into two categories:

- hygiene and
- positive motivators.

Hygiene consists of those things which do not in themselves motivate people, but where the absence thereof will demotivate them. Curiously, while pay is the reason why people go to work, it is hygiene rather than a positive motivator. If you pay people below the going rate, they will be demotivated. However, paying them over a fair rate will not motivate them more. It can become counter-productive and wasteful.

The main positive motivator is recognition, the various ways in which you show someone that they matter to the business. Talk to them, congratulate them when they do well, be sympathetic when things go wrong. If may sound wet, but it works.

An efficient employee can achieve 40 per cent more than an inefficient employee. Setting performance targets to achieve efficiency can become counter-productive. In all but the most routine tasks, it does not allow for the varying degrees of attention matters can require. Too strict targets can prompt slipshod work. Give each employee a target, where possible, but be sensible in how you monitor it.

If you pay commission, keep the amount worthwhile but not too large an element of pay. Keep the commission structure simple, usually a single percentage rate. If you pay 3 per cent to a certain limit and 1 per cent above, you will soon find orders held over from one period to the next, or fictitious orders created in one period and cancelled in the next. Make sure that you reward what you want achieved. You do not want to pay commission for faulty production or orders from uncreditworthy customers or for difficult orders.

The law does not oblige you to have a Christmas dinner nor to provide free tea and coffee. However, it is usually advisable to do so. The motivation usually cost-justifies it.

Employee problems

Personal problems

If an employee starts to act out of character or admits to having a problem, it is advisable to provide some forum for him or her to discuss it either with you or with a suitable colleague. If the employee is of the opposite sex, it is advisable to offer him or her chance to discuss the matter with a colleague of the same sex.

Compassion and commerce are not mutually exclusive. While any business's scope for welfare is limited, you can often go a long way to help. The helped employee will be grateful and motivated, as may his or her colleagues. Colleagues are ideal people to help with personal problems, as you know them well but are not involved with them on any continuing basis. Many personal problems can be helped by commercial disciplines. For example, a divorce is simply a commercial negotiation once the emotions have subsided.

If an employee has a problem with drink or drugs, insist that he or she deals with it or be sacked. And only give one chance.

Troublemakers

Every employee will have an off-day. Everyone has funny ways. The most saintly person will occasionally get rattled. Unless the matter is very serious, you should shrug off such vagaries of behaviour.

Never let nonsense get a hold in your business. The first sign of any work-to-rule or non-co-operation must be stamped on mercilessly. However disruptive the consequences are at the time, such a problem does not go away and will become worse if you leave it. In most cases, straight talking will suffice. Do listen to genuine grievances and seek to resolve them. However, make it clear that you will not tolerate any trouble-making. If an employee is determined to cause trouble, give a verbal warning, a written warning and then, if it doesn't stop, the sack.

If employees fall out, don't try to make them friends again, just insist that they work together normally. Shouting abuse usually justifies a warning. Fighting justifies dismissal.

Incompetent best

A problem in all businesses is the employee who does his or her incompetent best, is not awkward or lazy, just slow or dim. No satisfactory solution has ever been found for the incompetent employee. Probably the best approach is an honest, but sympathetic one. See if the job can be simplified, or the person moved or trained. If none of this works, you must make a hard decision of whether to retain the employee. Do not let emotion cloud your judgement. If the answer is that he or she must go, do it as graciously as possible. You will still be as popular as a pork pie salesman at a barmitzvah, but you do not go into business for popularity.

Blunder

If someone makes a serious blunder, give a reprimand, but leave it at that. To ignore it will undermine your authority. Curiously, justified reprimands are positive motivators. They show the employees that they matter.

If an employee takes a reasonable risk which backfires, do not discipline someone who will already be disappointed. You do not want to discourage him or her from taking more reasonable risks.

Dismissal

The law

There are two offences relating to dismissal:

- unfair dismissal and
- wrongful dismissal.

Unfair dismissal is where you dismiss someone for an improper reason. Wrongful dismissal is where you dismiss someone by a wrong method, such as giving insufficient warning or no notice.

There is no time limit for wrongful dismissal, nor for unfair dismissal where the reason is discrimination, pregnancy or trade union membership. For other unfair dismissal cases, the person may only claim if he has worked for two years and does at least 16 hours a week. If he works for between eight and 16 hours a week, he can claim only after five years. Unfair dismissal cases are heard by an industrial tribunal. Wrongful dismissal cases are heard by the county court. They are a breach of contract.

Redundancy is always a fair reason but an employee may argue that this was not the reason. Note that redundancy applies only where there has been a diminution in that area of your business. It does not apply simply because you no longer need that employee. A redundant employee is entitled to tax-free redundancy pay.

Types of dismissal

An employee may be summarily dismissed for a serious offence. This means that the employee is dismissed from that moment and is not entitled to any compensation whatever. The exact scope for summary dismissal has not been defined, but has included violence, theft and a complete refusal to work. Note that in the final analysis an employee can simply refuse to do his job (under Trade Union and Labour Relations Act 1974 s16). And you can summarily dismiss him.

A dismissal for misconduct or incapacity should usually come after a verbal warning and a written warning (according to ACAS guidelines). You should usually allow a person to explain their conduct, and to have a friend or adviser with them. These steps considerably reduce the chances of the dismissal being held to be unfair.

Constructive dismissal is when you do not sack someone, but make life so unpleasant that they leave. This is held to be the same as if you had sacked them. Don't do it.

Difficult situations

It is fair to dismiss someone for criminal conduct, even outside work, if it could affect their work. An example is an accountant or storeman caught shoplifting. You do not have to wait for any court case, nor do you have to prove that the person is guilty. A dismissal is fair if you have reasonable grounds for believing that the employee was guilty.

If stock or cash goes missing and the culprit cannot be identified, you are allowed to dismiss the entire shift or even the entire workforce.

If staff pilferage is going on in a shop, it is quite likely that employees will have a good idea who is doing it. Announce that if the culprit is not identified, all staff will be sacked and give an out-of-hours telephone number for confidential information.

If workers go out on official strike, you can dismiss them all, but you must not dismiss some nor re-employ any dismissed person for three months. If it is an unofficial strike, you can pick and choose whom to dismiss.

Overview

Staff are frequently your most important asset. Look after them, motivate them. Involve them in the business. Be fair. Be kind without being weak.

21 Marketing

Nature

Marketing is more than advertising or selling. In its widest sense, it is the whole area of how you present your business, how you endear customers to your business. It covers how quickly you answer the telephone, how your product is packaged, how queries are dealt with. Marketing need not be expensive. Indeed the best form of marketing, personal recommendation, costs nothing.

Preliminary considerations

The preliminary considerations of marketing are:

- know your market
- see yourself as a supplier of a service (even when selling goods)
- keep your business under review
- review your market
- review your competitors.

Know your market

The best source of new customers is existing customers. Customers actually like buying accessories and related products from an existing supplier. A man who sold units for heat-sealing bags, realised that this was a 'one-off' supply. He started to sell the bags as well, and made a fortune.

Check to see that your market is what you think it is. A precision engineering company realised its market was educational establishments. It started to sell other educational items and increased its profits sharply.

Supplier of a service (1)
All businesses are supplying a service. You are not selling oranges, you are providing an outlet for people to buy them at a convenient place at a convenient time. A tailor offers a measuring and recommendation service. These areas may prove to be where you can score highly. It follows from knowing your market, to know what they like about your service. That can be promoted, improved on or expanded in scope.

Supplier of a service (2)
Ultimately, all goods are services. A food-seller is supplying nutrition and taste. A clothes-seller is supplying warmth, decency and fashion. When you sell a drill, you are actually selling holes in things. Understanding this allows you to look at those aspects of your product which are of particular importance to your customers. It lets you see where your product can be enhanced. It can also show where you can save costs by dispensing with inessential items. Is that fancy packaging really necessary, for example?

This approach also opens up a second tier of competitors. The seller of car shampoo is not only competing against other sellers of car shampoo. He is competing against the local car-wash. They are both selling clean cars.

Keep your business under review
The fact that there is a market today does not mean that there will be one tomorrow. Do you know anyone who still uses a record rack? It is well-known that Lucozade was originally just another soft drink. It was then marketed as a nutrition aid, because of its glucose content. Sales soared. Robertson's Jam realised that adults were losing their sweet tooth, and so started making a less sweet jam.

Review your market
At the very least you should know:

- how many customers comprise the top 80 per cent of your sales?
- how much of your profit does that represent?
- how much profit do you make from each product?
- how much profit do you make from supplying your smallest customers?

The answers to these questions may surprise you. You may find that only three customers account for 80 per cent of your sales, though you regularly supply over 50 customers. You may find that your big customers demand such big discounts that they account for only 20 per cent of your profit. You may find that one product makes a loss while another makes a big profit.

These answers allow you to identify those areas where you need to concentrate your efforts. For example, suppose a big customer accounts for 50 per cent of your business but only 10 per cent of profit, while small customers who account for 5 per cent of turnover, account for 15 per cent of your profit. The big customer can be told that his discount is to be reduced, knowing that even if you lost him, you would almost certainly be able to recuperate the loss from small customers.

Big companies engage in formal market research. This is usually a waste of time and money, simply telling the company what it already knows to another decimal place. It is also often wrong. However, some form of research is necessary. Many statistics can be bought 'off the shelf'. Do not become obsessed with 'target markets'. Products as diverse as chocolate, pens and dictionaries have almost the entire UK population as a target market. The idea that a small market is better is one of the absurdities of some marketing theory. The bigger the market, the bigger your potential sales. Only if the product is limited in appeal, such as software for a particular computer, do you need to consider target market sizes and how to reach them.

Always consider new markets. Children are not the only market for sweets. Schools are not the only market for educational books.

Review your competitors
Always keep aware of what your competitors are doing. If they are limited companies, obtain their accounts and reports from Companies House or through a credit reference agency. Obtain their catalogues. Possibly buy their products or use their services, to see how they are doing. Keep a cuttings file of anything relevant to your business. You may consider engaging the services of a cuttings agency.

The product or service

The first question
Whatever you are offering, there is an alternative. It may not be a direct alternative. The first supplier of computer games was competing with television, books and games. Identify the alternative and ask yourself why should someone buy your product or service rather than the alternative.

This is the Unique Selling Point (USP) of your product. Do not be tempted to make false claims or exaggerate genuine ones. Sometimes the USP is simply doing something better. Hoover did not invent the vacuum cleaner, nor Singer the sewing machine, HMV the gramophone, Frigidaire the refrigerator nor Kodak the camera. They just did it better, and their name became the household word. The opposite happened to Biro who did invent the ballpoint pen, but whose company has been beaten by Bic and others.

If your product or service is identical to others, as will usually be the case with a shop, you compete on related services.

The price
There is a mathematical procedure for fixing the optimum price. It involves interpolating empirical data into the formula $R = ax^2 + bx + c$ and then using differential calculus. It is not widely used. In reality, the optimum price is simply the highest price a customer will pay. This may be by reference to the price of competing products or by reference to how much the customer will save or earn by using it. The latter is known as 'cost-justification', which simply means spend

£X if you save or earn £X + £Y. But note that cost-justification is always a subservient factor to competition. The first pocket calculators cost more than £100. They could easily cost-justify themselves at that price. But no one would get away with selling an ordinary calculator for that price now.

Price is also influenced by the state of the market. This is known as 'feast and famine'. This states that stale bread is worthless at a feast but priceless in a famine. The optimum price is that at which you get the greatest profit. The law of diminishing returns states that the higher the price, the fewer items you will sell.

Suppose experience says that you will sell these quantities of widgets at these prices: 100 at £10, 80 at £11, 60 at £12, 40 at £13.

Which price do you use? You cannot say because we do not know the profit. The turnover of the sales is £1,000, £880, £720 and £520 respectively. Suppose the cost of each widget was £8: the profit for each option becomes £200, £240, £240 and £200 respectively. The optimum price is around £11-£12.

A last factor on price is that cutting the cost has the same effect as increasing the profit, but without reducing sales. Suppose you could cut the cost of the widget to £6: the profit becomes £400, £400, £360 and £320. The optimum price is £10- £11.

Advertising

The principles
The steps in planning your advertising are:

* write good 'copy'
* choose the right medium
* choose the right time and frequency and
* monitor the result.

Good copy
Good advertising copy traditionally is named after Verdi's opera *Aida*:

- it attracts *Attention*
- it arouses *Interest*
- it creates *Desire*
- it stimulates *Action.*

Unless you are particularly skilled in this area, leave this to a professional copy writer.

Right medium
All advertising media work. But which one works best for your is a matter of received wisdom and experience. Let an agency provide the former while you accumulate the latter.

Right time and frequency
If you know your market, you know its seasonal variations. It is obvious that more ice-cream is sold in summer than winter. It is less obvious that a third of a jeweller's sales are made in the six weeks before Christmas.

Repetition usually magnifies the impact of advertisements.

Monitor
Try as far as possible to monitor which advertising media are most effective for you. It may be possible to ask customers 'How did you hear of us?' All coupons should be marked so that when you get them back, you can identify when they appeared and where. If quoting an address include 'Dept XYZ/123' [or whatever] as part of the address to achieve the same result. Do remember to collate and report this information.

General promotion

The clearing banks are notorious for spending fortunes getting new customers, then doing everything they can to lose them with high charges, hidden costs and poor service. Marketing should look at all areas where the customer is influenced.

Packaging
Does your product lend itself to being supplied on a 'blister pack' (card with a cellophane coating)? This is suitable for retail domestic sales, but may be resented as wasteful if supplying a trade.

Telephone response
How long does it take for a customer to speak to the person he wants? It should normally be no more than 30 seconds. Does the accounts department know that?

Public relations
There is plenty of opportunity for free advertising through providing stories to the press, particularly the local press and specialist magazines. Other forms of public relations (PR) include sponsorship of local events, prizes for schools and fêtes and suchlike.

Public image
A good image can be made by how you present yourself. Smart premises, well-lit customer areas, a ready supply of coffee and a good telephone manner all help.

Selling

Selling is the discipline of shifting what you have in stock. It is much narrower than marketing. It should be understood that the salesman's job is not to take 'specials'.

A good salesman needs the discipline to understand human nature, sufficient knowledge of the product he is selling and the determination to complete a sale. The salesman should try to sell as much of his product to a customer as possible. If a firm sale is not possible, try to get an indication of when a decision may be made. As a matter of control, salesmen should routinely report how much time they spend in face-to-face discussion with potential customers. Watch any salesmen. They can easily run away with the expenses. Do not let the salesman quote excessive discounts. If he justifies an order on the grounds that you should accept its prestige value, tell him he will be paid in prestige.

22 Cashflow

Cashflow statement

The cashflow statement analyses your flow of funds in and out of the business over time.

For example, suppose you accept an order for £10,000 that will take one year to complete. You must buy £2,000 worth of material at the beginning and pay £400 a month in labour and other direct costs. The job makes £4,400 profit and is worth having as you are currently only making £300 in net cash inflow. You start with £1,000 in the bank and an overdraft limit of £1,200.

The cashflow is:

	Jan	Feb	Mar	Apr	May	Jun
b/fwd	1,000	(1,100)	(1,200)	(1,300)	(1,400)	(1,500)
in	300	300	300	300	300	300
out	(2,400)	(400)	(400)	(400)	(400)	(400)
c/fwd	(1,100)	(1,200)	(1,300)	(1,400)	(1,500)	(1,600)

	Jul	Aug	Sep	Oct	Nov	Dec
b/fwd	(1,600)	(1,700)	(1,800)	(1900)	(2,000)	(2,100)
in	300	300	300	300	300	300
out	(400)	(400)	(400)	(400)	(400)	(400)
c/fwd	(1,700)	(1,800)	(1,900)	(2,000)	(2,100)	(2,200)

The order is profitable – if you get as far as completing it. By February, you have used all your funds and reached your overdraft limit. The bank will start bouncing your cheques.

A business does not go bust because it is making a loss. It goes bust because it cannot pay a bill when it falls due. A cashflow statement, such as the one above, finds when you need cash and how much. This can be presented to the bank manager as a mini-business plan, to make sure you have adequate facility.

Discounted cashflow

When the period extends into years, you may want to allow for the cost of capital or inflation. You determine the rate you may want to use.

Suppose your 'cost of capital' (how much it costs to fund your business, such as bank interest) is 13 per cent. You need to apply discount factors to each year's cashflow. The discount factor for year 1 is 100/113 = 0.8850. For year 2 it is 100/113 multiplied twice = 0.7831. For year 3 the fraction is multiplied three times, and so on.

For example, a machine costing £11,000 will produce income of £2,500 in each of the next six years. That is a total income of £15,000 against expenditure of £11,000. That is £4,000 profit isn't it? Let us see. Here is a discounted cashflow (DCF) statement.

Year	Cashflow	DCF factor	Discounted cashflow
0	(£10,000)	1.000	(£11,000)
1	2,500	0.8850	2,212.50
2	2,500	0.7831	1,957.75
3	2,500	0.6931	1,732.75
4	2,500	0.6133	1,533.25
5	2,500	0.5428	1,357.00
6	2,500	0.4803	1,200.75
	5,000		(1,006)

Allowing for inflation, the machine loses £1,006 over the five years.

Credit control

The two elements of credit control are:

- preventative – avoiding bad debts and
- curative – recovering debts.

Avoiding bad debts

Prevention is better than cure. A customer wants trade terms for an order worth £20,000 on which you make £4,000 profit. If you accept it and he pays, the order is worth £4,000. If you accept it and he does not pay, you lose £16,000. The moral is that any decision about creditworthiness is weighted against the customer. That loss of £16,000 could end your business. Don't risk it.

If the customer is a slow payer, he is incurring a cashflow advantage at your expense, as explained above. If the customer is a household name like J Sainsbury, or Marks & Spencer, there is no real risk. If the customer is the government or a local authority, you will be paid, eventually and after much bureaucracy. Otherwise ask for:

- a bank reference and
- two trade references from 'nationally known companies';

and check them up with a credit reference agency.

Details of the bank reference must be sent to your bank who will ask the customer's bank for a report. This comes back in a coded message such as 're J B Ltd, considered good for the figure mentioned'. This means that the company is satisfactory. The message 'the bank has serious doubts about the customer' means do not give credit. The trade references usually are just a brief satisfactory statement, but do read them. The credit reference gives details of anything registered about them, such as the times they have been taken to court. Remember that there is no such thing as a good credit reference. The best situation is an absence of a bad reference. Some banks now refuse to give references or impose conditions.

Do not give trade credit to an embassy or anyone with diplomatic immunity. You cannot sue them and they know it.

Export customers

For overseas customers you need to be particularly careful. Normally, you should ask for a 100 per cent irrevocable 30-day letter of credit drawn on a London bank.

- '100 per cent' means that all the money is payable
- 'irrevocable' means that the customer cannot cancel it
- '30-day' means that you are paid 30 days after supplying the goods
- 'letter of credit' is where the bank pays you on submission of the correct documents proving that you have supplied the goods
- 'drawn on a London bank' means that you do not have to trust a dodgy foreign bank.

You should also seek credit insurance through ECGD.

You quickly learn which countries are uncreditworthy. You learn not to be impressed by relations of Saudi princes. Most of these lessons, you have to learn the hard way. If a customer offers to buy £1,000 worth of goods on an unconfirmed letter of credit drawn on a Nigerian bank, you should consider blowing £1,000 on riotous living. The effect on your business will be identical, and you will at least enjoy the latter.

There is a foreign exchange risk if the customer is paying in his own currency. There will certainly be losses when the currency is exchanged. There are ways of hedging such a loss. Your bank can explain them.

Recovering debts

Getting customers to pay their bills is a demanding job needing persistence, patience and politeness. Send out your invoices and statements promptly. Deal with any queries quickly, even those you suspect as being time-wasting. The most effective way of extracting of payment is persistent and polite telephone calling. The most obdurate bought ledger clerk and her boss will yield eventually. For a regular supplier, stopping supplies can be effective. But that is a strategy that cannot be used too often and may backfire even then.

Do not make any threats unless you really intend to carry them out. If you have to sue, use the county court for debts up to £5,000. It is a simple, quick and cheap procedure. The most you pay is £70 to service a summons on the debtor. That is added to what he owes you. Also, by serving a summons, he becomes liable to interest from the date he should have paid. A booklet from the county court gives full details of how to serve a summons.

If the summons is contested, a private pre-trial review is held. If the summons is ignored, a judgement can be obtained by default after 14 days. The court gives a judgement which becomes a black mark against your customer's credit rating. But you still do not have your money. The judgement can be enforced by sending in the bailiffs to seize his property (but they have no right of admission); distraining his property; attaching his earnings or bankruptcy/liquidation.

The Small Claims Court can be used for sums up to £3,000 (prior to 1 January 1996, £1,000).

23 Special circumstances

Going from employment to self-employment

Summary
If your employer offers you the chance to continue working but in a self-employed capacity, you should consider the advantages and disadvantages carefully.

The advantages are:

- you are your own boss
- you pay tax under the more favourable Schedule D than Schedule E
- you pay less national insurance.

The disadvantages are:

- you lose all employment law rights
- you are excluded from being a member of any occupational pension scheme
- you must keep your own records
- you lose all rights under a contract of employment (such as sick pay and holiday pay)
- you must negotiate your own pay and chase up your invoices for payment
- you may be laid off at very short notice; note that sometimes the reason for offering self-employment can be an underlying insecurity in the business.

The following paragraphs will help you evaluate whether to proceed. But remember, only you make the final decision. Remember to consider the section on 'pay rate' below.

Whether self-employment will be accepted
Because self-employment confers considerable tax and national insurance advantages, Inland Revenue and the Department of Social Security are reluctant to accept that someone is self-employed. There is no point in 'becoming self-employed' if it is held that you are still employed for tax and NI purposes.

There is no simple formula to decide whether someone is self-employed. You can always present your case before Inland Revenue. If necessary, you can go to appeal on it. Guidance is given in the leaflet *IR56/NI139 Employed or Self-Employed?* available from Inland Revenue and Social Security offices. The relevant part reads:

If you can answer 'yes' to the following questions, it will usually mean that you are **self-employed**:

- Do you have the final say in how the business is run?
- Do you risk your own money in the business?
- Are you responsible for meeting the losses as well as taking profits?
- Do you provide the major items of equipment you need to do your job, not just the small tools which many employees provide for themselves?
- Are you free to hire other people on terms of your own choice, to do the work that you have taken on? Do you pay them out of your own pocket?
- Do you have to correct unsatisfactory work in your own time and at your own expense?

If you can answer 'yes' to the following questions, you are probably **an employee**:

- Do **you yourself** have to do the work rather than hire someone else to do it for you?
- Can someone tell you at any time what to do or when and how to do it?
- Are you paid by the hour, week, or month? Can you get overtime pay? Though even if you are paid by commission or on a piecework basis you may still be an employee.
- Do you work set hours, or a given number of hours a week or month?
- Do you work at the premises of the person you are working for, or at a place or places they decide?

Income tax
The main advantages of Schedule D tax over Schedule E are:

- you are allowed to claim more expenses (they do not have to be 'necessary')
- you pay the tax later
- the basis period method gives you a cashflow advantage and can reduce your tax payable
- you can avoid tax for work done overseas
- the costs of obtaining work are allowable under Schedule D, but not Schedule E
- you can claim capital allowances.

National insurance
You pay Class 2 and Class 4 national insurance instead of Class 1. Your 'employer' pays no national insurance. As explained in chapter 10, the maximum NI paid by the self-employed in the tax year 1998/99 is £1,411.15. Suppose you were an employee earning £26,000. You are liable to pay the maximum of £2,256. Your employer is liable to pay £26,000 x 10% = £2,600. The total paid is £4,856. By becoming self-employed you save 37.5 per cent. Your employer saves 100 per cent. Together you save 71 per cent.

However, you lose these benefits:

- unemployment benefit
- statutory sick pay (but not sickness benefit)
- statutory maternity pay (but not maternity benefit).

The position regarding contribution requirements for different social security benefits is:

Benefit	*Class 1*	*Class 2*	*Class 3*
unemployment benefit	yes	no	no
sickness benefit	yes	yes	no
statutory sick pay	yes	no	no
invalidity benefit	yes	yes	no

maternity allowance	yes	yes	no
statutory maternity pay	yes	no	no
widow's payment	yes	yes	yes
widowed mother's allowance	yes	yes	yes
widow's pension	yes	yes	yes
SERPS	yes	no	no

Employment law
You lose the following employment rights:

• wrongful dismissal
• unfair dismissal
• redundancy
• minimum period of notice
• maternity leave
• leave for public duties, ante-natal care.

And you lose these rights found in most contracts of employment:

• paid holiday leave
• paid sickness leave.

You may also lose the right to use social and other facilities. You become ineligible for any company pension scheme and for the state-run SERPS. In addition, you must invoice for your services. Companies tend to be more dilatory at paying invoices than paying wages. You must negotiate any increases as a contractor. You could find your 'employer' less sympathetic to an increase than if you were an employee.

Pay rate
All the disadvantages above can be compensated for in contracts and pay rates. Remember to do so. The loss of paid holidays and other absence, and the increased provision you should make for pensions and sickness, mean that you should expect your self-employed rate to be about 50 per cent more than your employed rate. If your earn £10 an hour, you should aim for £15 an hour as self-employed.

Other points

Remember to register for class 2 national insurance. Keep a set of books. If you become a limited company, appoint an auditor and complete the relevant paperwork. Monitor your income against the VAT registration threshold.

Buying an existing business

General

When you buy an existing business, you save the expense, time and risk of having to build up a business from scratch. Businesses are advertised regularly in publications like *Dalton's Weekly*, *Exchange and Mart* and Tuesday's edition of the *Financial Times*. The sale may be handled by an accountant or solicitor.

Value

The value of a business is a matter for commercial judgement and negotiation, just like buying a car or house or anything else. Don't be afraid to haggle. As a guideline, the purchase price usually has two elements:

- net assets
- goodwill.

The net assets are the physical things you take over: buildings, furniture, machinery, stocks etc. The fixed assets' value will be a fraction of what they would cost to buy new. The fraction reflects how old they are.

Goodwill is more nebulous. Basically, it represents the value a business has because it is already trading. If you believe that it would take you six months to get a new business to the same level of trade, the goodwill would be part of six months' profits. In reality, it may be between one and four years' net profits.

For example, a shop has the following:

1 saleable stock which cost £10,000
2 unsaleable stock which cost £1,000

3 new counters etc which cost £4,000
4 other fittings which are halfway through their life, and would cost £8,000 to replace
5 repairs which the landlord requires and will cost £2,000
6 two years left on a five-year lease at £20,000 a year. The current rent would be £30,000
7 an annual profit of £40,000.

You might value the shop as:

1 saleable stock at value £10,000
2 unsaleable stock ....nil
3 new counters..£4,000
4 other fittings, half of £8,000 ....£4,000
5 repair bill outstanding ....(£2,000)
6 lease premium 3 x £10,000...........................£30,000
7 goodwill on profit, say 1 year at £40,000......£40,000
                                                                    £86,000

Remember that the price you actually pay is a matter of negotiation. There is no need to cost out each element in this way, but it can be useful for negotiation purposes. The 'goodwill' element is the most important element.

Always remember that you should only buy the goodwill that you acquire. For example, a hairdresser can acquire much personal reputation and following. That will go when you take over his business. A grocer is likely to have much less personal reputation and following. It may be necessary to protect your goodwill by clauses in the transfer contract which stop your seller setting up in business too near or too soon.

Franchises

Nature

A franchise is an arrangement whereby a franchisor allows franchisees to use his patent, trade marks, trade names, experience, etc to set up their own businesses in return for a fee.

For the franchisee, such an arrangement is particularly attractive as much of the uncertainty and risk is removed. In particular, the franchisor:

- will have established criteria for determining where a business should be located, and the broad principles by which it should be run
- will provide you with some training
- will know how to provide the service or goods and
- will know the most effective way of marketing it.

Franchises include many household names, including most oil companies' petrol stations, Kall Kwik printing, Dyno Rod, ProNuptia, and Wimpy. There are other advantages. For example, the franchisor may be able to negotiate good quantity discounts, and pass the benefit to you with promotional literature already printed. The franchisor may also be able to provide cover to mind the business in your absence. He will certainly be able to advise you.

Advantages and disadvantages
The main advantage is that a franchise removes risk and uncertainty. It is almost a halfway house between employment and self-employment. You still own the business, but have much of the decision-making with attendant risk and effort removed. As a franchise is usually for a defined area, you have the added security of knowing that the franchisor will not set up another business near you. This does not stop another franchisor or another independent business doing so, but it does provide a limited territorial security.

The disadvantages are:

- you do not have a full say on how your business is run
- you will probably need the franchisor's permission to sell the business (and remember that the goodwill is more his than yours) and
- you must pay a franchise fee. This is often a single entry fee and an annual fee. The entry fee is not tax deductible.

Observations

Franchises have a good record of staying in business. The household name franchises all seem to be run fairly, allowing the franchisee opportunity to make good profits and enjoy the freedom of self-employment.

As with any other continuing contractual relationship, it is essential to check out the other partner and to satisfy oneself about the equity of the contractual terms. A check can usually be done simply by talking freely with existing franchisees. The commonest complaint from franchisees is over having to pay the fee after a few years, by which time they have all the skills they need and resent still paying. However, a more realistic view is that few franchisees would actually have done as well as that without the franchisor's support.

Franchises can go wrong. Horror stories have appeared about unscrupulous franchisors. But franchises tend to have a much higher success rate than other types of business.

Management buyouts

Management buyouts (MBOs) arise when the workforce of a company decide that they can run the business better than the existing management. It should be stressed that all workforces think this, but they are not always correct. There is also the management buy-in whereby a workforce buys another business. These tend not to be so successful.

An MBO is an acquisition of an existing business (see above) with the advantage that all the staff and expertise are in place, and now with the added incentive of owning the business (and thus owning its shares). The most successful MBO is probably National Freight Corporation, which was bought out in 1982. The biggest was Gateway Food for £2.4bn in 1989. Other household MBOs include MFI/Hygena, Magnet and Reedpack. In 1989 West Midlands Health Authority management services division became the first public sector MBO.

MBOs are very popular with venture capitalists, who will lend more money and at better terms than for an equivalent start-up. As with all contracts, there must be a willing buyer and a willing seller. The buyer must be you and your colleagues who share a common vision, get on well and are commercially minded. Your employers must wish to sell. This often happens after a takeover. The new management want to rationalise the business by selling off bits that do not fit into the new structure. A management buyout quickly gives its members part of the action of a big company. How to go about this and what to do is generally beyond the scope of this book.

Non-profit making organisations

Non-commercial organisations include charities, churches, public sector bodies, professional bodies, military bodies, social and sports clubs, political bodies and trade unions. Even though they do not exist to make a profit for their members, that changes very little in practice. Such organisations should still have targets, still prepare budgets and still follow basic management disciplines. Too often charities are run by failed businessmen, churches by clergy with no commercial experience, clubs by those who are popular, and societies by those who have proved themselves in a different field. This is a recipe for disaster, and disaster is often what confronts such bodies.

Most organisations still need to acquire money. While that may not be its main target, it will usually be one of them. Staff should be treated in the same way as employees, even if they are volunteers. Their commitment is the substitute for cash; nothing else has changed.

Most non-profit making organisations are exempt from income tax and corporation tax. There is no general exemption from VAT, though there are some minor specific reliefs which benefit charities.

24 When things go wrong

Introduction

All business involves risk. If you take enough risks, you will have some go wrong, however well managed your business is. The first thing to understand is that there is no shame in having a failure on your hands. Walt Disney went bankrupt twice before becoming a multi-millionaire and founding one of the world's biggest and most successful businesses.

As money is the language of commerce, any problem in business is ultimately a financial one, and a cashflow problem. Every business problem can be solved with cash. The problem may be part of a successful business venture or it may be that the business is collapsing round your ears. If the latter, you are unlikely to want to read this chapter then, so read it now, however optimistic you feel.

In an extreme case, you may have to end the business. This is an unpleasant task. You are destroying your dream. It is the nearest you get to killing your baby. But those who have had this unpleasant task have often been galvanised by it to greater determination and greater skill. They can often become successful leaders of new businesses.

Priorities

Stopping the bleeding

When things go wrong, you are in the business of damage limitation. You need to think through your priorities. If someone is bleeding badly, the first priority is to stop the bleeding. Similarly, if you are losing money, stop that loss as quickly as possible. If part of your business is losing so much money that it is likely to bring down your whole business, shut it down. Stopping the haemorrhaging of cashflow is more important than replacing it.

If you are stuck in a lease, talk to the lessors with a view to ending the lease. If the lease is for tangible property (such as vehicles and furniture) and you go bankrupt, they will not only lose your future rental payments, but could also lose the property as well. The lessors are in business. You may be pleasantly surprised at how sympathetic they are to your position.

Generating cash
The next priority is to get your hands on as much cash as possible. You must also quantify your indebtedness. This is an unpleasant experience, but essential. If people owe you money, chase them hard. It is your cheapest source of finance.

It may be possible to borrow money, but the problem is that this is 'distress financing'. If the business is in that much trouble, you will not be able to borrow on the strength of the business and will have to pledge security. If you go to a private financier, he will only invest on recovery terms. He is likely to drive a very hard bargain. It may be possible to borrow interest-free from a close relation or friend. Doing so is a matter of personal judgement, but remember that all loans carry an interest charge. The interest charge here may be in the form of moral obligation or submission which can be worse than paying interest.

If you have assets, consider a sale and leaseback arrangement. You sell the assets to a finance company and they lease back to you. It does not matter what the assets are, nor how exclusive they are to your business. This gives you a capital sum when you need it in return for regular payments under an ordinary lease.

It is tempting at such times to cash in life insurance policies or to borrow against pension funds. Try to resist this. These are designed to fund tomorrow's problems. A pension fund is protected from your creditors, however serious your position becomes. Don't remove that protection.

If you still have something to sell, consider a special offer to bring in quick cash. Set a time limit of perhaps six weeks, when you will give an extra discount. Make it worthwhile. You can always tell your customers that it is to 'fund expansion of the business' or to 'strengthen the business's position'. This can be worthwhile even if you must sell items at a loss. Remember a business fails because it cannot meet its cashflow, not because it is making a loss.

Creditors
The other step is simply to declare a moratorium. You tell your creditors that you have hit a problem period and cannot pay their bills on time. If you are honest with your creditors, pay them something and offer them a schedule for repaying the rest, you may be surprised at how reasonable they are. Debt collectors are usually sympathetic to a business in trouble, but only where the proprietor is honest and co-operative.

Sometimes it is possible to get the creditors to accept a smaller sum in full and final settlement. Under contract law, this does not usually relieve the debt. If you put a pistol to a creditor's head and say, 'I owe you £1,000; you can either have £800 now or nothing later', the law of estoppel usually allows the creditor to accept your offer and still claim the balance.

Making a small payment, perhaps of 10 per cent and offering to pay the rest in four equal monthly instalments will usually be acceptable. Exceptions are Customs and Excise who are always unsympathetic about any problems. Inland Revenue are more reasonable. They are reluctant to allow arrears of tax to be paid in instalments, though it can be achieved. In 1992, the then Treasury Minister Francis Maude, MP said, 'Inland Revenue does not pursue that [tax] in a blind and dogmatic way. If tax is owing and payment on the due date is impossible, the Inland Revenue will discuss payment over a specific period of time to meet the liability, and any taxpayer who is in difficulty in paying his or her tax should consult the Inland Revenue at the earliest opportunity to discuss how the difficulty might be resolved.'

Staff

Staff are always a heavy expense in any business. It is unlikely that a business with many staff can pull through a severe trough without losing staff.

Be honest with your staff. If they are properly motivated and feel that your business is 'their business', they will co-operate. When Walt Disney ran out of money making *Snow White*, his cartoonists agreed to work for no pay because they believed in what they were doing. If you have a good relationship with your staff, tell them the truth. You may find that they are willing to work for a reduced rate in return for a share of profits when the sun shines again. However, if you have to cut hours or lay off staff without agreement, do so. In difficult times, you must be single-minded in getting out of difficulty.

The bank

Tell the bank the truth about your position, but be positive in how you express it. Present your position as a problem solved, rather than just a problem. A problem will almost certainly increase the overdraft and may even require a loan. Bank managers are more concerned about an absence of news than bad news. Keep your bank informed.

Yourself

Remember that you are your biggest asset. Do nothing which impairs your ability to cope. In particular, avoid feuds and contentious litigation. If you must sue somebody, only pursue it vigorously if the outcome will save you. Otherwise, start it and then let the law take its natural progress (dead slow or stop). Do not become involved in anything that will distract you from recovery. But achieve a balance. Occasionally a high spot or social function will help keep you going.

The disciplines of human skills in chapter 18 become particularly important. Do not let the matters submerge you in a sea of despair. Approach the matter in a logical fashion, setting attainable targets as you go. In particular, stay positive and believing in what you are doing. At such times, you quickly discover who your friends are. You will probably be surprised by those who are sympathetic and those who are unsympathetic. Drop the unsympathetic, even if they are your immediate family. You do not need vexations to your spirit.

If you need help, do not be afraid to ask for it. Most people in business will have experienced some of what you experience, not that all are willing to talk about it. Social services and the church tend to be left-wing and unsympathetic to businessmen who get into difficulty. If you feel the need to the talk to the Samaritans, do so. Do not underestimate the value of simply 'unloading' your problems. Ultimately, all the problems one can experience boil down to a lack of cash or a lack of love. Business is solely concerned with the former. Do not depress yourself with the latter.

Recovery

One of two things will happen; your business will recover or will become insolvent. If it starts to recover, be careful because this is a very dangerous period. Patients convalescing after a serious illness start to feel better and can believe they are more recovered than they are. In consequence they over-exert and end up ill again. A similar situation can happen in business. You start to prosper again and believe that the business is fully recovered when it is not.

Insolvency

Nature
The worst that can happen to a failed business is insolvency. This arises when your liabilities exceed your assets. In itself, insolvency has no significance. If your creditors are willing to tolerate the situation, you can remain insolvent indefinitely without impediment. Insolvency becomes a disability only when someone decides to take action.

An individual can become bankrupt. The aim of the bankruptcy law is to give an insolvent person a second chance while trying to be fair to his creditors. They are given all that reasonably can be given, and then the slate is wiped clean. This can seem unfair to creditors. If a man is owed £1,000, why should he be paid off with, say, £500 and no more, even if the bankrupt subsequently becomes well off?

Before bankruptcy laws were passed, an insolvent person would either rot to death in prison or commit suicide, and the creditor received nothing.

A limited company is liquidated. This differs from bankruptcy in that the price is the death of the company. The liquidator sells off whatever he can lay his hands on and pays the creditors. A company can also go into receivership or administratorship. A liquidator is an undertaker, a receiver a cannibal, an administrator a doctor. A receiver may keep part of a business going with a view to selling all or some of it. An administrator keeps the business going under new management.

Steps in bankruptcy

Insolvency proceedings can only be brought by the person or company itself, or by a creditor who is owed at least £750. It is usual for the creditor first to obtain judgement from the court that the debt is due. This is not strictly necessary, though to proceed without a court judgement is generally rare. The main exception is when your loan to the creditor is 'secured'. This means that the creditor has the right to seize specific property to have his debt paid. A common example is a mortgage, when the mortgagee may seize the property and sell it to repay the loan.

Other than secured creditors, bankruptcy proceedings do not start until summonses arrive. These can be challenged or paid off. It is quite easy to 'buy time' on summonses if that is to your advantage. Having obtained judgement, bankruptcy is only one way of enforcing it. A creditor may be reluctant to proceed too far. The creditor is paying the expenses of bankruptcy (which can be heavy), with no guarantee that he will get all or any of his money.

The next step is that a bankruptcy petition is issued. If the court is satisfied that the petition is justified, a receiving order is made. You are still not bankrupt. Your property passes into the possession of a court officer known as the Official Receiver. You are allowed to keep bedding and clothing, and tools of your trade worth up to £250. Your pension fund cannot be touched.

The Official Receiver asks your creditors to provide a proof of debt. He also interviews you privately. From this he produces a statement of affairs – how much you have and how much you owe. He also checks to see if you have been fraudulent and whether it is likely that you have any money squirrelled away. He calls a meeting of your creditors. You may propose a 'scheme of arrangement' whereby you meet all or part of your debts. This scheme must:

- involve paying at least 25 per cent of the debt
- be accepted by at least 50 per cent of the creditors by number and
- be accepted by at least 75 per cent of the creditors by value.

If no satisfactory scheme is agreed, there then follows a public examination about your position. From this the court decides whether to make you bankrupt. If it does, it makes an adjudicating order. You are now bankrupt. A trustee, usually an accountant, is appointed.

The consequences of bankruptcy are:

- you cannot obtain credit (or try to) for more than £50 without disclosing that you are bankrupt
- you cannot be a company director or be involved in running a company
- you cannot hold public office such as a magistrate, MP or councillor
- your bankruptcy is recorded by credit reference agencies
- (in practice) you cannot run a bank account and
- all money you receive goes to the trustee to pay your trustee after allowing you a reasonable amount for living expenses.

The creditors are paid according to a set order.

If your bankruptcy arose from a hazard of trade and you co-operated fully in the bankruptcy, the court will probably decide that the provision of automatic discharge should apply. That means that your bankruptcy is discharged after three years. The impediments are removed, any debts still unpaid are wiped away. Otherwise, you must apply for your discharge which may not be granted.

Compromise

A company liquidation follows a very similar procedure to bankruptcy except that the consequence is that the company ceases to exist. The liquidator is required to comment to the court on whether the directors were guilty of wrongful trading, fraudulent trading or of obstructing the liquidation. If they were, the directors can incur penalties, including being disqualified from acting as directors for a fixed period (up to 15 years) and becoming personally liable for the company's debts.

Footnote

Even if you become bankrupt or your company is wound up, it is not the end of the world, just the end of that business. You will understandably feel low, possibly bitter. However, the law is designed to allow you a second chance. You now have valuable experience bought at a high price. Don't waste it.

25 When Things Go Well

When things go well, there are two main guiding principles:

- do not become complacent and
- look for a way of realising your dreams.

However big a business gets and however successful it has been, it is never immune from pressure or failure. Of the first 100 firms in *Fortune*'s top 500 in 1956, only 29 were still there in 1992. RCA and Pan Am were both once regarded as leaders in business acumen and innovation. They have both gone.

As a business expands, so do its needs. Alan Sugar, founder of Amstrad, said that running a public company was just an extension of his former trade as a barrow boy. Perhaps, but a barrow the size of a battleship needs different management.

Probably the biggest change is that you must let go. You are no longer delegating control, you are relinquishing it. You are no longer managing workers; you are managing managers. C Northcote Parkinson noted the phenomenon of 'injelitis'. A company starts dying when it is finally properly organised. The company that is still alive is the one which is just about to have a reorganisation to get itself straight. In the meantime, the managing director apologises for the cramped conditions, lack of storage space and the fact that recent building work has yet to be painted.

Getting your reward

Ultimately, money has no value until it is spent. Having built up a successful business, you want a share of its worth. The traditional way of achieving this was 'going public', selling at least 30 per cent of the shares to the public through a merchant bank. If your business is worth £20m, you receive an immediate £6m and become an 'instant millionaire'. You can still own much or even most of the company.

There are some steps in between, such as selling a minority shareholding or even selling out completely to a larger business. A complete sell-out (takeover) is usually achieved on best terms when the initiative comes from the predator company.

Remember that all the biggest companies were once small. Marks and Spencer started by Michael Marks, a Polish immigrant, selling penny ribbons at a bazaar in the nineteenth century. (Thomas Spencer lent him the money to buy a stall.) Sainsbury's was originally a butcher who made his own pies. But while these companies grew over a century, Microsoft, the computer software company founded in 1975, was worth £13bn in 1992.

Your business could also grow to such a size, even within your lifetime. Good luck.

Index

INDEX

REGISTRATION FORM

To receive the free updates to this book, please complete the form below (or a photocopy) and post it to:

Management Books 2000 Ltd
Cowcombe House
Cowcombe Hill
Chalford
Gloucestershire
GL6 8HP

Your name ....

Address...

....

....

....